New and Selected Poems

New and Selected Poems

by

Thomas Hornsby Ferril

GREENWOOD PRESS, PUBLISHERS
WESTPORT, CONNECTICUT

To my Sister

LUCY FERRIL ELA

Contents

Part I   *The Long Dimension*

Part II   *What Keeps on Moving?*

Part III *American Testament*

* Awarded Oscar Blumenthal prize by *Poetry: a Magazine of Verse*, 1936.
† "This Foreman" won *The Nation*'s poetry prize, 1927.

Acknowledgments

Wɪᴛʜ respect to poems in this book which have been previously printed elsewhere the author makes grateful acknowledgment to *The American Mercury*; *The Atlantic Monthly*; *Folk-Say:* University of Oklahoma; *The Forum & Century*; Harper & Brothers for poems taken from *Trial by Time, Harper's Magazine*; *Hound & Horn*; *The Nation*; *The New Republic*; *The New Yorker*; New York *Herald Tribune: Books*; *The Pacific Spectator*; *Poetry: a Magazine of Verse*; *The Rocky Mountain Herald*; *The Saturday Review of Literature*; *Scribner's Magazine*; *The Southern Review*; *Space*; *The Yale Review* and to Yale University Press for poems taken from *High Passage* and *Westering*.

Foreword

T<small>HIS</small> volume of poems by Thomas Hornsby Ferril combines new poems with selections from his three earlier books, now out of print—*High Passage, Westering* and *Trial by Time.* The earliest date back to the early 1920's, when he was working for the Denver daily papers and writing considerable newspaper verse. About 1926, when he entered industrial work, he began to scale down his output to about six published poems a year. There has been little deviation from this schedule since. Most of the poems printed here are from this period. However, some earlier ones have been kept, so this book does represent, from first to last, a body of poetical writing covering almost thirty years.

The poems are not arranged chronologically. Originally, there was some idea of grouping them in sections according to treatment and subject matter, but that proved to be possible only on a vague and limited scale. The range of the poems was against anything resembling an exact classification. The third section, for instance, groups poems together that might be considered historical in that they derive from trans-American experience. But any attempt to make historical background a basis for grouping runs head-on into Ferril's personal sense of history, peculiar to nearly everything he writes. With him, history is participative; what has happened, or what might have happened, sheds the paralysis of the past and takes on the character of an immediate poetic realization. This focusing of past and present into one emotion seems sometimes to create an overtone of anticipation, a fore-shadowing of the future that is half prophecy. A contemporary love poem with no historical allusions may draw on as much history in his sense—and usually does—as a poem about Jim Bridger or some dressmaker's dummy found on a dump in an old mining camp. The three divisions of the book, consequently, are a compromise with an original design that the poems themselves refused to fit into, which is as it should be.

Some recent and some early poems have been placed together in the opening section, to serve as a sort of coda for the two themes, time and continuity, that have given Ferril's poetry its color, direction and individuality during the years since he began writing. Time and continuity may seem commonplace elements from which to develop individuality in poetry. Other poets have written about time and its effect on things ostensibly stable and permanent; writers as far back as Xenophon have paid homage to the power of renewal that gives continuity to the human spirit. But with most of them, such things are incidental and minor, reasoned reflections touched on in passing. In Ferril's poetry, they are fundamental and all-pervading, underlying and coloring thought, emotion, even instinct.

In origin, much of this may be due to environment. The plateau region of the Rocky Mountains has always had, for some strange reason, an intensely stimulating effect on the efflorescence of stock poetical pronouncements about everlasting hills and the earth abiding unchanged and unchanging. The record for generations has brilliantly corroborated and extended the application of the old critical note that the best British poets always wrote their worst poetry in Switzerland. The truth is that hills do change; they shift, alter shape, switch colors and textures; rivers flood, change course, dry up and cut new channels for themselves; grasslands gully out, silt up and saturate with alkali, wind-strip and bank into new grasslands a couple of counties away. This process has been noted often enough in books—Shakespeare's forty-fourth sonnet, for instance, or any textbook on geology—but reading or reasoning about it is not the same thing as having it happen visibly and persistently, until it becomes a part of one's inmost consciousness. People in the plateau area of the Rockies are exposed to it from childhood; they come to take it for granted, except when, as sometimes can happen, one of them develops into a poet. Then it turns into lines like—

Three granite mountain ranges wore away
While I was coming here, that is the fourth
To shine in spring to sunlight from the north.

The responsibility of a mature and genuine poet is to take nothing for granted, neither in the world around him nor in himself, which is why genuine poetry continues to be important; and scarce.

The sense of shift and instability in inanimate things is only a part of Ferril's basic concept. Complementary to it is his understanding (understanding is not the right word; as with the orenda-doctrine of the Iroquois Indians, there is no right word for it) of continuity in the human spirit. Man, through his power of self-renewal, is always more enduring than the mountains, and every renewal holds in itself the possibility of new growth and illumination and fulfillment. *En ma fin est mon commencement*—the old tapestry motto of Mary Stuart has an application that is timeless and universal. In the swing of time, the worst day is still some sort of threshold.

From this balance of opposites—transition and renewal—there comes a concept of something permanent: love. Not love in its ordinary romantic sense, but something wider, more resembling Keats's "spiritual excess," or Dante's *amor sementa*; the passion that perpetuates life and everything in it of permanent value—love of inquiry, of naming things, of communicating emotion and experience, of recognizing and giving form to material:

> Love of watching, recognizing, naming,
> Knowing why similar ash of men and cattle
> Leaves talismans that differ as a hymn
> Might differ from an idle opal mine.

The understanding of love as independent of time, beginningless and endless, is in such poems of the first section as "Blue-Stemmed Grass," "Words for Time," "The Prairie Melts." It reaches a greater elaboration in some poems of the second section, as in "Grandmother's Old Dear Friend," where the process of continuity brings truth and illusion into conflict and concreteness—

> Not wing, not womb, not charity half-anthem,
> Not the ninety-ninth lamb nor yet the hundredth lamb,
> Nor even blue woods wincing from the ice-cap
> Nor any island listing toward a hymn,

> But of them all essential—

A man has to know a country to draw on its landscape and life and history for symbols in developing themes such as these. Ferril knows the Rocky Mountain country better than anybody: so instinctively and intuitively that his increasing control of its symbols, past and present, has been less a search for directness in expression than what Mazzini called the march toward self-realization to which mankind, willingly or not, consciously or not, is in the long run committed. His knowledge of Western history, surer and more realistic because basically direct and firsthand (his family had reached the Missouri River as early as 1809, and soon branched out on the Santa Fe and California trails), gives his use of it the feeling not of some remote event with period costumes, but of something come from the past to happen over again, with none of its original meaning lost and a new and deeper one added. In his poetry, the past, as a great Uruguayan poet once noted, does not lie behind us, but ahead; living does not carry us away from it, but into a deeper understanding of what it was and what it is.

There remain the poems. They were written primarily to be read aloud, and Ferril's Library of Congress recordings of some of them do give them a depth and closeness of rhythm that the printed page misses. But even on the printed page, as stages in the achievement of a precise and far-ranging literary artist, they are well able to speak for themselves.

—H. L. Davis

I

The Long Dimension

The Long Dimension

The lava cools,
The blue ice comes and goes,
The forests rise and wander,
The boys spin wooden tops, the finches sing,
But never a maple cries to be young again,
Nor sediment of river turns to stone
With lamentation: *It should be otherwise* . . .

How gardenlike and without prejudice
Elaborates the teeming earth about us;
Dead lambs, dead serpents, dead arbutus petals,
The frames of children, Earth, how silently,
The frames of father warriors, silently,
Never a whisper: *It should be otherwise* . . .
For these are words
And words, a long dimension
Beyond the flaking of the linen lips
And poor bitumined tongues that leave untouched
The mortuary spices and the meats.

It's very strange:
Yellow without name falls from a tree,
A beast will go to sleep and seem to dream
The scentings of a twitch of history,
But ours, a longer loneliness to measure,
For a man is neither a maple nor a panther,
He can desire a woman,
He can desire an island,
He can make words for woman and for island,
His tongue can lose the count of stolen cattle
Remembering the taste of river mint;
His woman walks alone beside the ocean,
Feeling her substant hollownesses changing,
Speaking to poplars burning into winter
Syllables they cannot understand.

Trial by Time

Out of the old transgressions of the seas
We come,
Encroachments of the land,
No vestige of beginning,
No prospect of an end.

Salt of the blood is ocean bathing still
Each cell of brain and heart
Burning uphill.

Out of the tide-slime
Credulous we come,
Singing our latest God stabbed and perfumed,
Springing the eye of the enemy from the socket,
Building a ladder to a broken bird,
Meadow and mine to the pocket,
Dream to the word.

Out of the sluggard butcheries we come,
Cowering so at night in a white cold sweat,
Staring at hills and lovers,
Yet strange with a fairer courage,
To us of all beasts given,
To meet with flaking hair and nostril numb
The ice-long ice-long dream of peace on earth,
Somewhere on earth,
Or peace in heaven.

[5]

Who Are the Cousins?

Who are the cousins the mind makes?
How does a sand lily in a vacant lot
Give you the rose-glow towers, the miniver princes?
How can a cottonwood in the dusty rain
Give you the tap of a sandal in Argolis?

Time of Mountains

So long ago my father led me to
The dark impounded orders of this canyon,
I have confused these rocks and waters with
My life, but not unclearly, for I know
What will be here when I am here no more.

I've moved in the terrible cries of the prisoned water,
And prodigious stillness where the water folds
Its terrible muscles over and under each other.

When you've walked a long time on the floor
    of a river,
And up the steps and into the different rooms,
You know where the hills are going, you can
    feel them,
The far blue hills dissolving in luminous water,
The solvent mountains going home to the oceans.
Even when the river is low and clear,
And the waters are going to sleep in the upper swales,
You can feel the particles of the shining mountains
Moping against your ankles toward the sea.

Forever the mountains are coming down and I stalk
Against them, cutting the channel with my shins,
With the lurch of the stiff spray cracking over
  my thighs;
I feel the bones of my back bracing my body,
And I push uphill behind the vertebrate fish
That lie uphill with their bony brains uphill
Meeting and splitting the mountains coming
  down.

I push uphill behind the vertebrate fish
That scurry uphill, ages ahead of me.
I stop to rest but the order still keeps moving:
I mark how long it takes an aspen leaf
To float in sight, pass me, and go downstream;
I watch a willow dipping and springing back
Like something that must be a water-clock,
Measuring mine against the end of mountains.

But if I go before these mountains go,
I'm unbewildered by the time of mountains,
I, who have followed life up from the sea
Into a black incision in this planet,
Can bring an end to stone infinitives.
I have held rivers to my eyes like lenses,
And rearranged the mountains at my pleasure,
As one might change the apples in a bowl,
And I have walked a dim unearthly prairie
From which these peaks have not yet blown
  away.

Blue-Stemmed Grass

There's blue-stemmed grass as far as I can see,
But when I take the blue-stemmed grass in hand,
And pull the grass apart, and speak the word
For every part, I do not understand
More than I understood of grass before.
"This part," I say, "is the straight untwisted
    awn,"
And "Here's the fourth glume of the sessile
    spikelet,"
And then I laugh out loud at what I've done.

I speak with reason to the blue-stemmed grass:
"This grass moves up through meadow beasts
    to men."
I weigh mechanical economies
Of meadow into flesh and back again.
I let the morning sun shine through my hand,
I trace the substance bloom and beast have
    given,
But I ask if phosphorus or nitrogen
Can make air through my lips mean hell or
    heaven.

All that the grass can make for any beast
Is here within my luminous hand of bone
And flesh and blood against the morning sun;
But I must listen alone, and you, alone,
Far children to be woven from green looms;
We move forever across meadows blowing,
But like no beast, we choke and cannot cry
When the grasses come, and when the grass is
  going.

Words for Time

Ask a boy on his back
In a track the buffalo cut
How long it takes that cloud
To cross that butte.

How many turns of calico tied to a spoke
Of a wheel
Make a mile
Make a century?

Ask dew on the ox-bow:
Where did the century go?
Ask lantern light on the butternut sleeve
In the evening.

Tonight I was watching a jet-plane lag behind
The spokes of light a hub of sunken sun
Was turning in the under-West
Behind the Rocky Mountains.

The jet-plane, for an instant of twelve mountains,
Held its own with a span of apricot sky
But lost to a fanning blade of choke-cherry;
Nearer, a snow-white-pitch-black magpie bird
Sauntered the West wind faster.

What shall I tell the children about Time?
Children who never counted the sing-back sway
Of the shoes of a single-footer horse,
Surrey by goldenrod or pung by snow,
But know the red light from the green
And when to go
And go
And go so soon
Over and under the poles of the earth
And toss the earth like a toy balloon.

Shall I tell them Time is countable repetition:
Tree-ring, heart-beat, Ocean's coral accrual?
Shall I speak allegory: Time has teeth,
Forgives, is foolish, yawns, rubs like a river,
Is bald, is nick, is nurse, is pale avenger?

Big Time, small Time, war Time, your Time?
Hickory-dickory Geiger Time?
The mouse ran up the isotope,
Five . . . ten . . . fifteen . . . twenty . . .
Twenty-five . . . thirty . . . thirty-five . . . forty . . .
Where you are you shall burn up
In your hiding place or not!

I'll say those things for all those things are true,
And I will tell the children Time is Love,
Like a slogan to laugh at on a greeting card,
Like a One-I-Love song made of daisy petals,
Like bidding the mountains sloughing off to sea
Good wayfaring, my hills, goodbye, goodbye!

Let boys and girls grow old and die one day,
Well taught that Time itself does not exist
Where nothing can go faster than the light
That let me love that magpie's wing tonight:
Love of watching, recognizing, naming,
Knowing why similar ash of men and cattle
Leaves talismans that differ as a hymn
Might differ from an idle opal mine.

And I will tell them. . .
No, I'll let them learn it:
All constellations, bench-marks, citadels
Continuing and lost and starting over
Within a whisper: "Was it all right with you?"
Passion into slumber into being.

The Prairie Melts

The prairie melts into the throats of larks
And green like water green begins to flow
Into the pinto patches of the snow.

I'm here, I move my foot, I count the mountains:
I can make calculations of my being
Here in the spring again, feeling it, seeing . . .

Three granite mountain ranges wore away
While I was coming here, that is the fourth
To shine in spring to sunlight from the north.

A mountain range ago the sea was here,
Now I am here, the falcons floating over,
Bluebirds swimming foredeeps of the blue,
Spindrift magpies black and splashing white,
The winged fins, the birds, the water green . . .

Not ocean ever now but lilies here,
Sand lilies, yucca lilies water-petaled,
Lilies too delicate, only a little while,
Lilies like going away, like a far sound,
Lilies like wanting to be loved
And tapping with a stick,
An old man tapping
The world in springtime with a stick.

[14]

This buffalo grass? O, you who are not here,
What if I knock upon your tombs and say:
The grass is back! Why are you still away?

I know the myth for spring I used to know:
The Son of God was pinned to a wooden truss
But lived again, His blood contiguous

To mine, His blood still ticking like a clock
Against the collar of my overcoat
That I have buttoned tight to warm my throat.

Who was His lover? That might keep Him nearer.
Whom did He love in springtime fingering
All fruit to come in any blossom white?
Cupping His hand for tips of nakedness
And whispering:

"You are the flowers, Beloved,
You are the footstep in the darkness always,
You are the first beginning of forever,
The first fire, the wash of it, the light,
The sweetest plume of wind for a walled town"?

I light my pipe. A heavy gopher sags
Into her burrow scarfed with striping snow,
So quick, so slow, I hardly see her go.

Yonder, a barbed-wire fence, and I remember
Without intention how a wire can twist
A gopher hole until it burns the wrist . . .

And there are wrists like mine that hang in trees,
And overcoats like mine to mulch the stubble,
And there are houses where the young men say
It would be different if the harbors and
The looms were ours . . .
The end of women wailing for a ship.

But sundown changes day to yesterday:
The purple light withdraws from purple light,
The listing mountains close the lilies tight.

Above the blackness still one falcon burns,
So high, so pale, the palest star seems nearer,
One fleck of sun, one atom-floating mirror.

His shadow will not strike this world tonight:
There is a darker homing hollow bone
Of wings returning gives to wings unknown.

My tilted skull? My socket eyes? Are these
With chalk of steers apprenticed to the grass
When mountains wear away and falcons pass?

No answer is.
　　　　　No policy of rock
Or angel speaks.
　　　　　　　Yet there could come a child
A long time hence at sundown to this prairie,
A child far-generated, lover to lover,
Lover to lover, lover to lover over . . .
(O I can hear them coming, hear them speaking
Far as the pale arroyos of the moon.)

The child could walk this prairie where I stand,
Seeing the sundown spokes of purple turning,
The child could whisper to a falcon floating:
"I am not lost.
　　　　　　　They told me of this prairie:
This is the prairie where they used to come
To watch the lilies and to watch the falcons."

Basket

The children out of the shade have brought me
    a basket
Very small and woven of dry grass
Smelling as sweet in December as the day
I smelled it first.
              Only one other ever
Was this to me, sweet birch from a far river,
You would not know, you did not smell the
    birch,
You would not know, you did not smell the
    grass,
You did not know me then.

Wood

There was a dark and awful wood
Where increments of death accrued
To every leaf and antlered head
Until it withered and was dead,
And lonely there I wandered
And wandered and wandered.

But once a myth-white moon shone there
And you were kneeling by a flower,
And it was practical and wise
For me to kneel and you to rise,
And me to rise and turn to go,
And you to turn and whisper *no*,
And seven wondrous stags that I
Could not believe walked slowly by.

Mountains Themselves

Mountains themselves are plausible. You can
    look
At the ranges one behind the other folding
Into alien blueness with apparent meaning;
But you'll find you need a bird or something
    that
An old man said when you start to finish a
    mountain.

A thunderstorm's an early instrument.
I've used a mountain storm for germinating
The grasses down on the prairie and a sickle
Of lightning for harvest quickly, with wrinkled
    clerks
Down all at once in the city groping with
    pencils
Into decimals of wheat long after the arc lights
Have come on. I've done it quickly, often before
I've heard the thunder. Or you can wait for the
    thunder.

Or you can finish a mountain very slowly
With fans of light that mark the equinoxes,
Setting their red dials at the end of always
The same long street their special sundowns
   need
For remembering which of the front doors on
   the porches
Show in a year new scars of tacks from which
Were hung the ribboned wreaths of waxen
   death.

I have kept careful measurements of this
Since boyhood and prefer the slower way.
Some of the hills I've used are nearly finished.

Canter the Horses, Please

Country boy, I see you with your lantern
Swinging your giant shadow against the trees,
You're climbing the chokecherry draw where I'm
     always repeating
                    . . . *canter the horses, please* . . .
. . . words not making sense to a companion,
Might there be one, nor sense to mare or whip,
Some ritual like a child's I start and stop
With turgor of my lip against my lip.

I won't dismount, explain. You're someone else
Walking the same draw now, left shoulder west.
Is the world beautiful? The lantern light?
Something to chokecherry your throat's addressed?

Let there be ritual, sir, if you return
To this dark valley, warring years behind,
Something you started to say, don't understand,
And love and half recall and hope to find.

An Oak Leaf Fell

Up from the sea I shredded lightning from
My sleeve and knuckled thunder from my hair,
I walked a league but still you did not come,
I could not find you any anywhere;
I cut a hickory stick, I peeled it bare,
I climbed twelve mountains, I was very sullen,
I told a sky to whip a hawk and a mare
To dream, I hickory struck the heads from mullein,
Marigolds even, ere the night had fallen;
Then I beheld you, strolling and suspended,
Golden you were, powdered in clover pollen,
Closer you loitered until nothing ended,
An oak leaf fell, it stopped, it isn't down,
Many an oak tree, many a glacier gone.

Stem of Wheat

Some fifteen thousand times I've gone to sleep
Not certain yet when actual sleep begins,
And fortune may as imperceptibly,
If you have one, flake down your coffin roof
To dust your lips and be a hundred years.

How still you lie, neither to lilacs naked
Nor aware of snow or clocks or any mirror,
You do not move, you do not bless the islands,
You do not touch the river with your finger,
You do not press the window sill at seven,
No one can remember of your saying
Yes or *no* quarrelsome or generous,
There is no notifying twig or bench mark.

These pallid inventories and the pressure
Of the moon's arithmetic are on me as
We walk together down this summer night
And I, I think, am trying to persuade you,
Now you are beautiful, soon you'll be dead,
I'm rather sure I'm trying to persuade you
Because I am a man who has read books
Wherein the lover, unlike wren or stallion,
Allies himself with worms, his alternates.

I'm rather sure I'm trying to persuade you
And, questing so, I find myself confused
By having pulled this wheat stem from its
   socket,
I take the wheat stem and I walk ahead,
I leave you here alone, I don't return
Until I've wandered far enough to split
The midnight oceans with my hands to show
A wheat stem to incredulous far countries.

This Trail

We may have been coming up a misty spring,
A summer of long fire, some autumn when
Those mountains over there were first thrown up
To make a purple windrow, but we needn't
Talk of the breaking down of a skull or blossom,
Or whether the hair lives longer than the heart,
Or how improbable it always was
That we should ever walk this trail together.

This is no night for winding clocks. I love you.

II

What Keeps On Moving?

Judging from the Tracks

Man and his watchful spirit lately walked
This misty road . . . at least the man is sure,
Because he made his tracks so visible,
As if he must have felt they would endure.

There was no lovely demon at his side,
A demon's tracks are beautiful and old,
Nor is it plausible a genius walked
Beside him here, because the prints are cold.

And judging from the tracks, it's doubt-
    ful if
A guardian angel moved above his head,
For even thru the mist it can be seen
That he was leading and not being led.

Grandmother's Old Dear Friend

Grandmother's old dear friend, alert with wine,
Telling of bison knocking the clothesline down,
And there were grasshoppers in the early days
So thick you had to hoe them off the sun.

Only the wine tonight keeps the bison
    trundling,
Only the wine remembers the grasshopper hoe,
When your sod-luster talk has ceased, dear
    lady,
They will have gone precisely where you go.

Yet the enchanted ancestor, unreasonable
    enough
To tether townships to the harper's thumb,
Will keep his grave manured for flowers some
    longer,
Weeds preferring many another tomb.

For the dead, like bison, perish in some order,
All ghosts are delicate as coffin fern:
First perish the fiscal dead, then die dead
    priests,
Great slayers die more slowly in the urn

Yet early as the vast mechanic lovers
Who died of kissing continents to pieces,
Yet slow as never true practitioners
Of love: no thing gives up, no thing releases.

Not wing, not womb, not charity half-anthem,
Not the ninety-ninth lamb nor yet the hun-
    dredth lamb,
Nor even blue woods wincing from the ice cap
Nor any island listing toward a hymn,

But of them all essential, all there is
Of love, or was, or can be sung or guessed
As long as the sun comes up from the eastern
    ocean,
As long as the sun goes down behind the west.

Now Is Always Beginning

My blue tires wrack the Horse Creek bridge
At Meriden above Cheyenne,
What did they call that sumpter squaw?
Was it Molly-Picket-Pin?

My throttle opens Goshen Hole,
Who was Molly? Lilith either?
Which of them is lost in greasewood?
Which of them my mother?

Lilla Abi! Lilla Abi!
Lulla Molly lullaby....
Tongue can taste a myth forever,
Tongue can sing its meat and die.

The Hereford cattle blow away,
The books of Alexandria burn,
The gunsight peak the North star used
Is mummy flake, it won't return.

But Lilith, Molly-Picket-Pin,
Where I am the first man is,
You, Sheepherder I'm passing now,
You are, you start all mysteries:

Man and Woman, Hell and Heaven,
Valley, Mountain—Hand, Machine,
And there . . . the lights of Hawk Springs,
The first lights ever seen.

I let my index finger leave
The steering wheel to split the rock
Of the sea cliffs of Nebraska,
I wind and set their clock.

Noon

Noon is half the passion of light,
Noon is the middle prairie and the slumber,
The lull of resin weed, the yucca languor,
The wilt of sage at noon is the longest distance
    any nostril knows . . .
How far have we come to feel the shade of this tree?

Magenta

Once, up in Gilpin County, Colorado,
When a long blue afternoon was standing on end
Like a tombstone sinking into the Rocky Mountains,
I found myself in a town where no one was,
And I noticed an empty woman lying unburied
On a pile of mining machinery over a graveyard.

She was a dressmaker's dummy called Magenta.
I named her that because, all of a sudden,
The peaks turned pink and lavender and purple,
And all the falling houses in the town
Began to smell of rats and pennyroyal.

The town was high and lonely in the mountains;
There was nothing to listen to but the wasting of
The glaciers and a wind that had no trees.
And many houses were gone, only masonry
Of stone foundations tilting over the canyon,
Like hanging gardens where successful rhubarb
Had crossed the kitchen sill and entered the parlor.

The dressmaker's dummy was meant to be like a woman:
There was no head. The breasts and belly were
A cool enamel simulating life.
The hips and thighs were made adjustable,
Encircling and equidistant from
A point within, through which, apparently,
The woman had been screwed to a pedestal,
But the threads were cut and the pedestal was broken.

I propped Magenta into an old ore-bucket,
Which gave her a skirt of iron up to her waist;
And I told a mountain at some distance to
Become her lilac hair and face and neck.
It was the fairest mountain I could find,
And then I said, "Magenta, here we are."

And Magenta said, "Why do you call me Magenta?"
The sky no longer glowed rose-aniline,
So I looked at the town and thought of a different reason.

"Magenta's a mulberry town in Italy,"
I said, and she said, "What a very excellent reason!"
(I said no more though I was prepared to make
A speech a dressmaker's dummy might have relished,
About a naked Empress of France,
And how she held her nightgown at arm's length,
And named the color of her silken nightgown
In honor of the battle of Magenta,
The very year, the very day in June,
This mining camp was started in the mountains.)

The sun was low and I moved to a warmer flange
On the pile of broken mining machinery,
And Magenta said, "It's always afternoon
Up here in the hills, and I think it always was."

"Why always afternoon?" I said, and she answered:

"Mornings were crystal yellow, too hard to see through;
The realness didn't begin until afternoon;
We both are real, but we wouldn't have been this morn-
ing
Before the blue came up. It was always so:

Nothing real ever happened in the morning,
The men were always digging for gold in the morning;
They were dreaming deep in the earth, you never saw
them,
But afternoons they'd come up to bury their wives."

Magenta stared a moment at the graveyard.

"These women wanted me to be their friend.
I spent my mornings with them making believe.
They'd sit around me talking like far-off brides
Of things beyond the mountains and the mines;
Then they would get down on their knees to me,
Praying with pins and bastings for my sanction.

"Then they would look into mirrors and come back,
They'd look out of the windows and come back,
They'd walk into the kitchen and come back,
They'd scratch the curtains with their fingernails,
As if they were trying to scratch the mountains down,
And be somewhere where there weren't any mountains.

"I wasn't what they wanted, yet I was.
Mornings were never real, but usually
By noon the women died and the men came up
From the bottom of the earth to bury them."

"Those must have been strange days," I said, and I tossed
A cog from a stamp-mill into a yawning shaft.
We listened as it clicked the sides of the mine
And we thought we heard it splash and Magenta said:

"The men would measure in cords the gold they hoped
To find, but the women reckoned by calendars
Of double chins and crow's-feet at the corners
Of their eyes. When they put their china dishes on
The checkered tablecloth they'd say to themselves
'How soon can we go away?' When they made quilts
They'd say to the squares of colored cloth 'How soon?'

"They could remember coming up to the dryness
Of the mountain air in wagons, and setting the wheels
In the river overnight to tighten the spokes;
But by the time they got to the mountains the wheels
Were broken and the women wanted the wagons
To be repaired as soon as possible
For going away again, but the men would cut
The wagons into sluice boxes and stay.

"Each woman had seven children of whom two
Were living, and the two would go to church.
Sometimes the children went to the opera-house
To see the tragedies. They can still remember
The acrobats and buglers between the acts."

I spoke to Magenta of how the graves were sinking,
And Magenta said, "All this is tunneled under;
I think some of these ladies may yet find gold,
Perhaps," she sighed, "for crowns," and she continued:

"Maybe you never saw a miner dig
A grave for a woman he brought across the plains
To die at noon when she was sewing a dress
To make a mirror say she was somebody else."

"I never did," I said, and Magenta said:

"A miner would dig a grave with a pick and shovel
Often a little deeper than necessary,
And poising every shovelful of earth
An instant longer than if he were digging a grave,
And never complaining when he struck a rock;
Then he would finish, glad to have found no color."

I didn't know what to say to that, so I said:

"It's getting dark at approximately the rate
Of one hundred and eighty-six thousand spruces per
    second,"
And Magenta smiled and said, "Oh, so it is."

And she said, "Up here the men outnumbered women,
But there were always too many women to go around;
I should like to have known the women who did not
    need me."
She indicated that their skirts were shorter.

"And so should I," I said. "Are they buried here?"

Magenta said, "I think there were hardly any:
They came like far-off brides, they would appear
Each afternoon when the funerals were over.
Some disappeared, some changed into curious songs,
And some of them slowly changed into beautiful moun-
    tains."

She pointed to a peak with snowy breasts
Still tipped with fire and said, "The miners named
That mountain Silverheels after a girl
Who never was seen until along toward evening."

"This is an odd coincidence," I said,
"Because I've been using that mountain for your head."

From Saturday Evening On

A man on Deer Creek told me how he'd seen
Ned Corbin only Saturday afternoon,
But it was Tuesday now and Ned had been
Dead, he said, from Saturday evening on.

I'd seen Ned Corbin nail a shoe to a hoof,
I'd seen his cattle over in Douglas County,
I'd looked from Mount Deborah down on his red
    barn roof,
I'd read of his getting mountain lion bounty.

There are lilies and trout along his bend of the
    river,
You'd snag your fly on mullein belonging to Ned,
You'd have to include them all in any forever
He still could have among us now that he's dead.

Not that a man need outlive the set of a shoe,
Or go much beyond a dog that trees a lion,
If you start to fill in with lilies and mullein you
Are adding your design to his design.

Of course, if Ned had told me about the lilies,
Or if the mullein had made him recognize
Something he'd never thought of as being his,
It might hold on and keep its shape and size.

[42]

Some twenty-five thousand sunrises or so
Belong to a man of seventy before
People coming to town start starting to
Note and forget not seeing him any more.

In the store where Ned got mail they light the
    stove
With yesterday's paper naming more men and
    places
Than Helen and King Priam were speaking of
Gazing down from the wall at Achaean faces.

The neighbors were always going to remember
    Ned,
Some, if they hear it, know the name of Priam
Through teacher, school tax, something worthily
    said
Of love and agony over a long, long time.

A singular impact, atom to atom, goes
For Ned or you through light, through sense,
    through capture,
We argue back from lilies and from snows
To lion meanings, timelessness and rapture.

Solstice

Orion sprawls like a bullfrog up December,
The Star-Swan, winter-wounded, falls below
The icy West.
              I'm cold!
                         My dog is cold:
The nostril cauterized, the frosty ear
Cocked to the twang of tightening lake.

I trespass here:
A storage of the sun,
A lag of pasture light discharging slowly,
No nimble pumicing the cheek
To shape it boylike back.

Was there a sunflower ever?
Arm of the swimmer dripping the overstroke?
Mountains blue as cornflowers in the evening?

Being in summer here and the silver shag
Of cottonwoods a naked myth?

My dog is cold, my dog is very cold,
Within my glove my finger is not mine.

[44]

Some of the Boys a Little While Had Names

I speak of a street in Denver, Colorado:
Out of the distances of Summertime
Came teamsters under apricot parasols,
So high, so stately moving
On the great green beautiful elephant sprinkling wagons
Raking the dust with rainbow tines of spray;
You could smell a rainy push of cool and scuff
The thunderheads between your toes and wander
Over the cinnamon-silvertip Rocky Mountains,
Never returning.

There were autumns of jingle-bob cattle and swallow-
    fork cattle
Sloping out Downing Street,
Horses in sunbonnets, golden balls on the hames
Of the horse-collars,
And some of the boys a little while had names
As you'd name a sulphur-saffron star Arcturus,
Or name a child Joe Gans or Agamemnon,
Or name a nick a moon in an agate marble,
Discrete, distinguishable from the moon in the sky
As long as some could still recall the meaning.

But now there are no cattle passing by,
The crack of a drover's whip, if there were one
To crack a whip, would be phenomenal;
The moon is silence lighted by the sun.

The boys strode up the lion ramps and down,
They panted and they boasted and they rested
Paler than lily-white Pollux, lily-white Castor,
Handlebars under the trees like dappled antlers
Pleaching the moods of maple to box-elder
Until the trees, insensible to names
Of vests and watch-chains, golden vegetables,
Respected lusts and temperate honesties,
Quit being trees: there was no pollarding
For higher growth and slowly they came down
By fractures of mild tempests and new times.

You could ride your bicycle out Downing Street
To the very end where you had to make a choice:
You could go the way the cattle had to go
Or hook to the West toward Riverside Cemetery
Where people had to go, or you could be
Impractical about alternatives,
You could change the street each evening at the summons
Of tomorrow's candlepower by wick, by sun.

Sunrise Edition—1943

I'd like to edit a paper for Mount Massive:
Piltdown Man Co-stars with Veronica Lake,
Homer Tops Keynes in Declamation Contest,
Pliny Injured Lighting Lamp with Uranium,
Townsend Group Repeals Thermodynamics,
Zeus and Stalin Ousting Serapis,
FLASH—10:19 (between the last recession
      and second coming of ice to Bethlehem)
SITTING BULL DIES IN CHAIR AT SING-SING!
The condemned man, who had eaten a hearty
      breakfast,
Went to his doom refusing to recant
Alleged remarks in Gath to Sun Yat-sen:
Hydrogen's heavier than hydrogen.

Waltz Against the Mountains

We are waltzing now into the moonlit morning
Of a city swung against the inland darkness
Of the prairie and the mountains and those lights
That stab from green to red and red to green.

The music ends. We lean against the sill
Feeling the mountains blowing over us.

What keeps on moving if your body stops?

I ask you this as if we were not new,
As if our city were an ancient city.
I ask you this in Denver, Colorado,
With a moon for the year's end over your naked
    shoulder.

Denver is younger than a white-haired man
Remembering yellow gold up to the grass roots.
They tell of eagles older than Denver is:
I search the crystal edges of the twilight
For birds still floating over these prairies and
These mountains that had floated over these
    prairies
And these mountains when there was no city here.

[48]

I walk alone down Blake Street and Wazee,
Looking for asters growing through the hub
Of a wheel that brought my city up from the
  prairie;
But a welder's mask with purple eyes is hanging
From a peg in a wall where a yellow ox was tied
The night the people came in a wagon to rivet
The steel of a set-back tower to a set-back tower.

I was pulling hair from the trunk of a cottonwood
  tree
The longhorn cattle rubbed when a sudden man
Started tossing red-hot rivets up through the
  leaves,
Scorching the amber varnish of the leaves.
He made the red-hot rivets stick to the sky.
I had to quiet the glowing clatter down
The frozen silence of a long long time;
I had to leave the tree and look for another.

The prairie twinkles up the Rocky Mountains.
Feel how the city sweeps against the mountains;
Some of those higher lights, I think, are stars.
Feel how the houses crowd and crack uphill.
The headlands buckle with too many houses.
They're trying to find a place where they can
  stand
Until the red lights turn to green again.

I'm only half as old as the city is.
I'm younger than an old box-elder tree;
I'm hardly older than the old cathedrals,
Yet I remember primroses and yucca
Out there where all those houses are tonight.
We children gathered primroses and yucca,
We gathered sand lilies and cactus blossoms.

But there's hardly a child in all the sleeping chil-
    dren
From here to where we think the stars begin
Who sleeps in a room where a child, his father,
    slumbered.

When you wake in the morning tracing a drowsy
    maze
In the wall paper the sunrise trembles through,
The ceiling never whispers old directions
A ceiling learns from leading old men's eyes.
Off on that prairie frozen cattle flatten
With snow you cannot tell from moonlight on

Their shoulders and with darkness-clotted skulls
And darkness sagging in their hollow flanks;
And through those mountains black above this
    prairie
Are other animals alive and dead,
Some warmer than the rocks and some as cold,
And we are here, moving ourselves in music.

What keeps on moving if your body stops?

Mine is a city that has never known
A woman on a high wall looking down
Forever on the firelight of her kinsmen.
You're only a woman looking out of a window;
There are no ships, no smoking sacrifices,
And what we make, we are, and it is finished.

There's hardly time to speak beyond the flesh
In a city where the young men are always finding
A better place to start a cemetery.
Yet when this darkness cools the trembling tips
Of music in your breasts and earth has found
More certain use for me than waiting for
A woman on a wall, *what keeps on moving?*

We used to know, we don't know any more.
But I have seen enough of hills and blood,
And lovers and old men and windowsills,
The bones of churches and the bones of moun-
    tains,
To know how far we may have come together,
And where we're going for a little way.

So late you came up to these mountains from
A valley by the sea you hardly know
Yet where to gather blossoms of wild plums;
But part of what you are was here before
You came, and part of what you were is gone.
Already melting snow moves through your
    shoulder,
Atoms of hills are warm within your shoulder,
And somewhere in your fingers that press my
    fingers
Are particles of corn the bison made
When their bodies clogged the river in the spring.

You are a woman younger than the city,
You are a woman older than the city,
You are the mountains changing into woman,
You are a woman changing into prairie.

See how the moon goes down behind those moun-
    tains.
The hills with every waning moon are lower.
They cannot last. They go where we are going.
They wear away to feed our lips with words.

The moon's a sand lily petal floating down
Behind the blue wall of the Rocky Mountains.
I see you as a woman on that wall,
Stepping down crumbled distances forever,
One terrace of a mountain at a time,
One terrace of a prairie at a time,
Until you join your kinsmen at the sea.

What keeps on moving while the mountains
linger?

It may be something spoken at a window
About the uses of some hill we've borrowed,
Or something a welder sings to a cottonwood tree,
Or something the seasons make the lovers say
When it's summer on the plains and spring on the
    ranges,
And we follow weeks of lilacs up from the prairie
Into lost towns of the mountains and return
With lilacs when the hay is being cut.

Remembering a Red Brick Wall in Rensselaer

Once in the Zuni sky, my lap belted down
To keep me from falling up, the red came in,
The red kept coming in, it rattled like
A dew-claw rattle, rattled like a peach,
Like a mesa eighteen-thousand finger-printed
Down there
Roses.

I told the Zunis:
                    Let there be a grocer
Who always lives at Rensselaer, New York,
He always padlocks sundown to a red brick
    wall
As red as this red is.

Red as the mallows on the Kansas Waukarusha,
Red as the red the Greybull River gives
The Big Horn in Wyoming all the Aprils
All the centuries a fish is Jesus Christ
The Arno afternoons, the ember-golden.

I told the Zunis:
          Quandary to North Star,
Wild-rose mountains up the River Blue,
Forever-lover not amended by
A coffin spike
Or spoolings of disuse.

So did I speak to the Zunis from their Heaven
As the headwind slowed to fifteen miles an hour
And evening cooled the maize in the juniper
     valleys
And the great sun closed up many a grocery
     store.

Out in the Stovepipe Mountains

Out in the Stovepipe Mountains
A snowslide dropped like a piston of snow,
Slowed on a push-up of conifer air,
Then wracked and packed the trunks below.

It took a long time for the snow to melt
And a longer time to reach the sea
Through many a valley and many a valley
Where everybody had to be

Lonesome when the moon came up,
Lonesome for a far-off lover,
Lonesome for angels and whip-poor-wills,
Lonesome for roses and clover.

The valleys were strung like mandolins
Because the water ran downhill,
They cogged the cities to the sunny
Meadows green with chlorophyll.

And where bitumined cities nudged
Their oily turrets into whorls
Of peacock tails and pigeon breasts,
Men and women, boys and girls

Stared at the changeling water till
They changed to lads and maidens fair
Who lived a lonesome song ago
A hundred woods from there.

Where is my true love? Where is my youth?
The valley is worn a benchmark lower,
Arbutus atoms trail the shady
Atoms of men to the ocean floor . . .

And the sun is sluicing the oceans up,
And the Stovepipe Mountains are clouding over.

Kenosha Pass

You go in high gear to Kenosha summit:
That turquoise ocean lapping thirty peaks
Is hay now but the buffalo are dead.
The housing of your differential gears
Will break the gentians, but the Utes are dead.

Rime of the Passion of the Carpenter

Seven skies from anything
But mountains crunching mountains in
Until there was no sky at all,
I hugged a socket of canyon wall;

And far below, no wider than
A banjo string, a river ran,
Yet even deep down there so far
From goat or noon or calendar
I saw a pinch of dark I felt
Must be a place where a man had dwelt,
But whether hovel, cave, or shack
I had to know ere I turned back;
So back I zigzagged, up, around,
To find some way of getting down,
Yet now, the deeper down I went,
The higher climbed my discontent
With what my peeping, prying mind
Could find or hope or loathe to find.

I inched my muscle and my bone
Down ten black million years of stone
Until I reached the blindest pit
The undercutting river split.

And what I saw when I could see
Was a house of logs in front of me
That seemed, the more I stared at it,
Like a naked bride upon a bed:

The logs were beaver-silver, square,
No living thing but me was here,
Yet she was here with lips and face
That changed the canyon into lace
And curved the thunder-stammer of
The terrible river into love.

I turned to the river and counted ten,
Then stared at the silver logs again;
I asked how log chain, axe, and bar
Could fashion eye and breasts so fair,
And golden hair to seem so much
Like a house of logs a man could touch:
Great blocks of pine laid flat as brick
With passionate arithmetic
Undressing them, so smooth my eye
Walked up them like a butterfly,
And I smelled a rainbow of river glint
Like a hover of wet wild rose and mint.

Who built this house, I asked, why built
In a canyon cave of mica silt?

Every lintel was stroked and rolled
As if the adze and drawknife held
Some fingering influence as far
From clumsy tools as the evening star,
. . . every naked tenon clasped
In pitch as if a man had gasped
Some utter senseless ecstasy
To feel it fit so perfectly.

An olive hawk flew overhead.

"That's a hawk," the canyon said,
"This is granite, there's no sky,
This is a house two stories high,
The house is old and weathered white,
At noon these junipers are night
Except there where the lightning stung
One tree and left one shadow sprung;
There's nothing here, there's nothing human
Here but you, there is no woman."

But I thought of the dugouts lone men build
In the blackest canyons of the world
No higher than a man can shove
A plug of grass to sod a roof:
The ridgepole bellies and he'll crouch
The seasons dripping down his couch
Until his bed's a fungus bier;
But nothing like that happened here . . .

Skid and snub and spike and lever,
How could muscle work such timber?

The trees are burning through my hands,
My fingers cannot hold the rope,
There will be moonlight on your hair,
There will be moonlight on your throat.

I could almost hear and be that man,
I could stretch my hand and feel the span
Of caliper thumb to little finger
Racing over the rough green timber
As if to feel its beauty were
To touch the living soul of her,
Whatever far-off luminous dream
She may and must have been to him.

Yet he was alone, I know he was,
Working with hook and chain and truss,
Swinging his axe like a pendulum
Against the day when she must come.
I could hear the whipsaw make a love song,
I could hear the jack plane make a love song,
And I could hear him feel her voice
Echoing back when he made a choice
Between one bit to drill for a peg,
And another bit to drill for a peg,
Then see him watch her lovely face
Blessing him as he whirled the brace,
Jealous of every twig and blade
And lonely sound the canyon made.

A camp bird came so close to me
That I could look him in the eye,
Was there a bird today, my lover?
Where you were, did some bird fly over?

Yet I know this natural woman never
Came to love him by this river,
I know but for the circumstance
That changed these logs into a lens
I might have never seen her face
Nor felt the canyon turn to lace.

For deep in our confessed lust
For God in bits of thunder-gust
We feel, but darkly understand
The instrument within the hand
By which the woman . . .
Or the ape of blowing grass
In basket shape
Begins to be
And being is
More further than all mysteries:

And be there ashes, politics,
Wars recited, candle-licks,
Kings impending, panthers gutted,
Treasure ebbing, psalms rebutted,
All is far . . .
                    far sorrowing
Away . . .
                away from everything
When a man's heart cries: *I make it so*
Because I love you, love you so.

I Am the Horseman

I am the horseman you noticed across the prairie,
I am what made you say:
                    How beautiful
To ride so far away into the blueness . . .

Yet I have buckled one hole instead of another
In the throat-latch of the bridle of a horse
As if one hole in a strap were a doom or a sunrise.

And I have charged and overcharged until
They gasp with love and cry to stop, these ranges,
And slowed them to the lift of a coffin hinge.

Nothing you name is alien to these pressures:
The wars, the manifestos, distributions,
The old transgression of the grass across
The lovers and the skulls of lovers . . . nothing . . .
I scuff them down the prongs of rabbit brush,
All silvering the wind, all yellow gone.

The glance I give the twisting of a hoof
In the pennycress is as old a glance a man
Can give the earth.
                        Who has seen more a morning
Into battle or an evening coming home
Along Scamander or the Little Big Horn?
For who has changed the nature of a sunflower?
By what apportionment of blood? What whispering
Above the poised spear to split the breast?

Here in the loneliness of cottonwoods
Oh, I have overthrown the world with you;
I've propped your bleeding head, the last flag passes:

What is the meaning of the sagebrush now?
What is the policy of the councilors
Now if the crotch of a tree outgrows a boy?
If an old man stares at a falling leaf at sundown?

Lens for Plum Blossom

From tree to tree ahead of me
A thousand blackbirds flutter.
Then wheel their wings in synchrony
Like blades of a window shutter.

Blackbirds open, blackbirds close
The snowy woods: my steaming horse
Is breathing frost and swings his nose
Up the frozen watercourse.

Sundown notches the mountain gap,
I snatch a twig of cottonwood,
I stare at the sun through amber sap
That droops from an icy bud.

It isn't like a lens of glass,
Nothing that I see is clear:
Blur of bud and mountain pass
Over a horse's ear.

Yet staring so, not budged an inch,
I feel the white plum blossoms come
To blow against the saddle cinch
Shuddering winter-numb.

Life After Death

Down heaviness of winter flowers commingled,
Deeper we laid their bodies in the earth
Than storied levels of the living soil;
But I've come quickly home again from all
The many mansions of the coffin people,
Taking, in lieu of prelates, any elm,
The orders of the maples and the beasts,
The separate fragrances of separate flowers,
The prairie rattling in the summer lightning,
The mountains musical with purple timber,
The faces moving into any road,
Faces desiring, faces that remember;
And crowding graveside logic from my mind
To make room for the coat of a sorrel horse
Splitting the sunlight into shaggy rainbows;
And asking for this moment never more
Of any bird than that it cleave the sky.

I have come widely with my spirit over
The tombs of men, of prairies and of moun-
    tains:
I can distinguish with a clear precision
The summer bones of winter-frozen steers
From ribs of unicorns and jaws of centaurs;
I've changed no maiden to a mountain aspen,
Though I might take you to a dappled grove
Where graves are old and this is happening.

And I can tell you as a certain thing,
Still while events within our muscles let
Us swing an arm an arc of the horizon,
That you will love me more for having told you
To see what I have seen in natural men,
In elms, in falcons, or in coats of horses;
And I will love you more than beast or rock
Can love you, or the dead can ever love you,
If, with no special memory of this hour,
You say some day, because you have to say it:
    "Remember how it was when we turned our
        horses
    Out of the dark arroyo into the sunlight?"

That Afternoon

That afternoon, propellers roaring four,
His city sidled off and tilted over
A sorrel mountain swung like the mane of a horse:
He clucked down twice the cluck you make to the ghost
Of a horse in the last blue swale you walk him through
To work the trouble out and let him go.

No temporal or spatial congruence:
There was no horse.

                             He sat in a chair in the sky
As fast as he could with nothing going by
Except the very boy who is the young man
Who is very old, long dead and boy as one.

And mark, O sky, his stepping, meadow to meadow,
So certain, the vaster the grasses the lighter the shadow,
A hackamore in his hand, the rowels of
His spurs clotting with all the flowers of the earth.
Tidal meanders to the starry mountains,
Stalking an amber colt the gentians pounding,
And now, be it unreasonable, his palm
Has brushed a silken forelock as a wind
Might brush a primrose never touched by wind.

O muscular frolic sky, unlatched, so naked
Of age or ghosts or youth or youth forsaken,
Notice his fingers, practical as lace,
As practical for cottonwood as an axe,
And now the colt secured, be it unreasonable,
Mark how he tosses a pond around a stone
To make concentric oceans circle in,
Undulating, interlocking, closing
Upon a point of winter like waves of roses.

III

American Testament

American Testament

Where were their myths, if these were beautiful?
Was Daphne there, beloved of Apollo?

Kentucky was too dark and red with blood,
But Amos cut a path that Ruth could follow.

If these were bold in dreams, what Centaur's child
As fair as Jason ever led them on?

Job, in his bull-boat on the brown Missouri,
Slept while Ezekiel pushed a pole till dawn.

Calypso where? Was Niobe among them
With sorrow singing in her sons and daughters?

Isaiah, wounded by the Arkansas,
Heard Ezra's oxen drowning in the waters.

How were they beautiful without Diana?
Was there a valley of unwaking youth?

Jude took a squaw out of the Taos moonlight,
Joel bought a lover with a grizzly tooth.

If there was courage in their brutal being,
Was it not ugly gods that drove them on?

At eighty Daniel whistled hymns in Juarez,
And snow-white Joshua reached Oregon.

High Passage

What pure coincidences were the day the bee
Crossed the black river and came floating further West:
An old man felt no symbol streaming o'er his head,
But crushing English roses in his hunting vest
As if the flowers were there, spoke to his dusty son
Of this and that which he had written in his will,
And prattled on of England till the weary boy
Grew fearful of what lay behind each westering hill,
And watched horizons bobbing through the oxen horns,
Like circles screwed against his own identity,
Which thundered in his ears and through the wagon
    wheels
To roar beneath the silent passage of a bee.

The day the bee flew further West a Blackfoot girl
Laughed when her mother, mumbling of a buffalo bull,
Told of a maid that once a bull had wooed away;
Also that day a Ute boy topped a brown armful
Of wood with a gnarled snow-snake of the winter games,
Which now, in summer calm, could kindle evening fire;
So twilight fell across the world under the bee,
Whose flight sang down to peace, and while the moon
    rose higher,
The nodding prairie drowsed, for still unmeasured miles
Lay silent in the grass between the fires of those
Who trusting bulls would learn to fear a bee,
And lonely men remembering a droning rose.

Nocturne at Noon—1605

Walk quietly, Coyote,
The practical people are coming now
Into the juniper, into the sage arroyos,
Where the smoke is sweeter than anywhere
And the mud is ready for building
The city of Santa Fé.

While the Puritans over in England
Are getting ready to whisper,
There is a way and we will build a ship,
People in motion are looking at the sage
And seeing where the yellow goes in August
In all the violet sage and silver sage
Along the Rio Grande,
Not that they need the yellow on a faring,
But knowing where it is
And what hills are behind it,
As gulls know where an ochre billow beats
On something that is rock.

Coyote, on the silver road of Spain,
Stalk in the noon, the little mice are dozing,
While you are panting, evening comes to Spain,
Darkens the sculptured rats in Tarragona,
Closes the last Sevillian marigold,
Blackens the windows in Our Lady of the Sea,
And the sailors' sheds grow dim in Barcelona.

Be soft, Coyote of the noon,
Far to the east here is an evening that
Is more than many nights:
This evening, for the first time in the world,
Will Shakespeare leads a madman to his heath
Against the wisdom of a patient fool;
This evening, for the first time in the world,
The little hoofs of Don Quixote's nag
Start striking fire from flinty roads of Spain,
A little trot today, some salty grass,
The first star and the last pale cloud are set.
The cloud is over England, Lear is ebbing
Into the northern lightning of the air;
Somewhere there is a storm, my Sancho Panza;
The star is sinking in the Rio Grande,
Where Cradle Flower with teeth white as a beaver's
Laughs at her lover, Medicine of Corn,
Weaving his body through a hoop of osier.

Be still, Coyote in the noon,
You cannot see the sinking of the star
Into the burnt slit of the Rio Grande,
At noon, Coyote, stars are frail as pollen,
But Lope de Vega's gone to bed,
Philip the Third has gone to bed,
And the child Velasquez sucks his thumb
In the blackness of Madrid,
But Will Shakespeare hasn't gone to bed
And over England lightning flashes,
Soft, Coyote, Lear is mumbling
Into the northern wind.

Quick! To the south, Coyote, look!
Is it a rabbit in the noon?

No hare, Coyote, those are ears
Of a mule that comes up the deep arroyo,
Ears in the grass on the edge of the mesa,
Up comes the head, it's the head of a mule;
O soft, Coyote in the noon,
Oñate comes up the deep arroyo,
Rides up the silver road of Spain,
Juan de Oñate's over the edge now,
Stare, Coyote, at Oñate,
Have you seen a peacock plume before?
Or a spur as heavy as two young turkeys?

Still, Coyote, see his face,
For the mud is ready for building now
The palace of Santa Fé,
See the faces red and black behind him,
The practical people are coming now,
The Mother of Christ rides up the mud,
There's another friar on the left,
They're up on the silver sage again,
They see where the yellow is again,
The mud is ready for making walls
Where the smoke is sweeter than anywhere.
Be still, Coyote in the noon,
The practical people come.

Jim Bridger

Jim had a body that one morning took
A long pole in its hands and with a cry
That no one can remember strangely pushed
A hundred springing rivers down to mope
In folds of yellow sleep below St. Louis.
That afternoon the muscles of his body
Threw enough of the Rocky Mountains down so any
Of the oxen could step over them. That night
Jim Bridger's body cooled off in a cornfield
Where some day Kansas City was going to be.

Look at Jim Bridger standing in the cornfield:

What can you say to the old man in the evening
When the Rocky Mountains are coming back around
    him
Chanting a long blue tomb-song for his body?
What can you say to the old man in the evening,
A blind man standing in a field of corn
With the taproots waiting to lace his moccasins
Where Kansas City's going to be? Can you ask him:

"How do you know the moonlight on your hand
Is Idaho? How do you know the wind
Is Colorado coming to cool your armpits
When your arms have reached too far for loneliness?"

They let him ride a plowhorse to the cornfield,
But the horse has gone away and the dog has gone.
Jim Bridger rode Grohean, the Comanche stallion,
But Grohean is dead, he's out there in the mountains.
Do you know how a stallion falls in a water course,
With the neck curved back too flat and the ribs too high?
What can you say to an old man in the evening
When he gets down on his knees to feel the stubble
And feels with his hands the particles of earth
Binding Missouri together under the moon,
Binding Missouri to the members of his mountains?
What can you say when he lies down in the stubble
Staring too long as if his lids were lenses?

Will you remember him, Missouri River,
The boy with starlight on his shaggy head?
Do you remember him, New Mexico
The shaggy head in the mirror well of Taos?
You, Canada? You, white Mackenzie River?
You, grasses and blue flowers rimming the Arctic?
You, silver gulls of Utah, flying in
The wake of plows as if the plows were ships?
Nebraska, wooer of rain, will you remember
A cloud like a level rain cloud over two
Horizons and a tall boy moving like
A thunder master into the bison vapor?

You, Colorado, wrinkling out of an old sea,
Into the granite and the orchids and the high wind,
Where do his moccasins slip down hill in the needles?
Montana, when you lie on your back like a woman
Hearing the flutes of the Blackfeet over October,
Do you hear his name among the sorrow bringers?

Wyoming, in the morning when the world
Is turning over like a wheel and the mountains
Are tossing up golden rivers to every ocean,
How do you know which sea to give a river?
Do you remember anyone who told you?
You wide Dakotas, listeners of wind,
Where do the river namers stop at noon
For shady antelope against their tongues
With fifty songs to go into the sunset?

Sometimes, when I've quarreled a long time with Jim
    Bridger
For lying dead too long under a cornfield,
And never leaving the cornfield like a myth
That will not stay in any place too long,
I say: "Jim, you're ten consonants and vowels,
You're only the name of a lake in the Yellowstone,
And something the postmaster knows in the Clark's Fork
    Valley."

But I know why Jim will never rise from the cornfield
And walk a thousand miles to wake his stallion.

For I know how hard it would be to make a myth
When I hear Wyoming singing to the seven reeds
That quiver on a turbo-generator's breast . . .
When I write an advertisement and believe it
And watch the people believing my advertisement . . .
When I hear a city rocking at night to the same song,
Every night the same song, always the same song.
And I know why Jim will never stalk the moon
When I listen to people buying automobiles,
And what they say when they finger a fender curve,
When I listen to some of the things they talk about
Before they build high buildings and afterward
When they look up out of their windows at high
    buildings;
And I know why old Jim Bridger in the cornfield
Will always stay there until he isn't there.

So much for old Jim Bridger, but if you ask me
Where am I going on a summer day,
I'll tell you I am gathering instruments
About me like the seven reeds that quiver
On a turbo-generator's breast.
I'll tell you I am going to crack it out
From Denver to Taos, figuring about
An hour for a sandwich over Raton Pass.
I'll be in Castle Rock in thirty minutes
Which I would say was more than old Jim Bridger
Could make in a long day riding any stallion;
It will be dark from Cimmaron to Taos,
And I'll be tired enough to feel
Some of the instruments slipping away:
I'll feel the wheel dissolving in my hands,
And I won't be knowing about the brakes and throttle,
And the same song that makes the cities rock together
Will be moving through my fingers and the spruces,
But I won't know there's music in my fingers;
I'll be a slow thing moving into Taos,
Slow as Jim Bridger on a weary stallion;
But when I get to Taos I'll start over,
I'll feel the instruments and they will feel
Like something waiting for me in a cornfield.

Fort Vásquez

I've tried it slower but I think it's better
To be going fifty miles an hour or faster
When you pass by those low adobe walls
Builded by Louis Vásquez on the Platte
A hundred years ago. You pass them on
The motor road from Denver to Cheyenne.

This Louis Vásquez led the fur brigades,
He was Jim Bridger's partner many years,
They wandered on these prairies and these mountains:
If you take the skeleton of a cottonwood leaf
And call the stem the long Missouri River
And the other bones of the leaf the other rivers—
The Yellowstone, the River Tongue, the Big Horn,
The Stinking River and the Rosebud River,
The Wind, the Chugwater, the Sweetwater—
That's where they roamed, but one leaf will not hold
Their rivers on the other side of the mountains.

They built their walls the way the beaver did
Of river mud and golden river grasses,
And of these walls this beaver hunter formed,
Three walls are gone. The earth is almost level
Where they stood.
              The fourth mud wall, no higher than
The barbed-wire fence a rancher built to keep
The people out, still leans upon the wire,
And the windy barbed-wire cuts it like a saw.
A pace away flashes the whirring pavement,
Behind the pavement is the railroad track,
Where fireweed glows against a bank of cinders.

A long-haired buckskin man was Louis Vásquez,
And a handsome man who had driven a coach-and-
    four. . . .

Last night a magpie crossed the hunter's moon,
And I said:
          "There's a feather for you, Louis Vásquez,
To wear in your hair when you walk alone in October,
A feather, if you meet an Arapaho girl
In the yellow cottonwoods."
              Those cottonwoods
Were yellow puffs that trundled away as far
As I could see, like yellow tumble-weeds
Piling against the rose and indigo mountains;
But the magpie flew away and the long-haired man
Was dead, and a hundred prairie years were gone,
And I was making only some of the words
That yellow trees and hills have made before.

But getting back to why I like to pass
These crumbling walls at fifty miles an hour:
I nearly always go this way with men
Who have to know some science for their business;
They always tell me things I do not know,
And it's a road I'll want to travel more
Until I'm surer of each curve it's making,
And where the people go who turn at crossroads.

I've passed Fort Vásquez when the telephone poles
Were whipping by at the rhythm of my heart,
And listened to the driver's quiet story
Of fighting colloids in a filter press.
Sometimes we shuffle pairs of chromosomes,
While the mountains slowly turn and change their places.
(Mountains will follow as a new moon will.)
They whisper: *Do not listen to the driver!*
Tell him the old things we are telling you!

And within a bow-shot of where Louis Vásquez
Stretched out his buffalo robes on willow branches,
The whole binomial theorem clattered down
As something that would work all right until
You tried to make its logic alter Nature.

Another time when we were roaring by
To try to help the farmers fight the drouth,
We talked about the way the guard cells work
For photo-synthesis in the blowing leaves
In the barbed-wire fields on either side of the road.
(The barbs are tufted spindles wrapped in fleece
From sheep and clematis that press against them.)
And when the road was blocked by a tide of sheep
We spoke no more of photo-synthesis,
But I thought of the unseen vapors from the sheep
Charging the air with something for the leaves,
Even as dissolution of their bodies
Must charge the earth with something for the roots.

And what is happening is happening
To roots and leaves that split adobe walls.
You dead Arapahoes in the silent meadows,
We spent that wide green summer's day upon
A picture chart showing your prairie sun
Lifting a fountain water from every leaf,
But the syllables and symbols were our own,
And coming home we wandered among planets,
And filled the road with particles of light
That bounced against the car like summer hail.

So goes this road, but when we near these walls
The driver usually says:
                    There's old Fort Vásquez;
Somebody ought to put a marker there!
And someone says:
                    It ought to be restored!
And I'm about to say:
                    How beautiful,
With what you know of earth and air and flesh,
To let these old walls go the way they're going!
Let's bid them godspeed and be on our way!

Or I'm about to say:
                    How might we best
Unwind a hundred years? How might we now
Reorganize these elements again
With certitude that those who pass this way
Experience alone the works of Vásquez,
And nothing that our different hands have added?
But by the time the driver ends his plea,
Something has come and gone and come again,
And our feet are pressing hard on the floor again,
And talk begins again, perhaps of women.

There's something I am giving up to tell
You this, and if you turn your head away
When I say words like photo-synthesis,
Can I say more than *Are we here or aren't we?*
Shall we turn back? Is there some other road?

O I will not forget the measured sagas
Of older wayfaring across this world,
We'll keep them too. We add to what they are.
If you have time some night I'll sing you a song
About a loping crescent of Cheyennes
Moving under the moon toward Louis Vásquez;
I'll make a song about John Jacob Astor,
And all his warriors fighting in the mountains,
Or a song about a shadow in St. Louis,
A shadow warm with wine and honeysuckle,
And Louis Vásquez stepping out of the shadow
Into the silver laughter of the lovers;
I'll make a song of an island near St. Louis,
And gentlemen shooting each other down
With perfumed ribbons pinned against their hearts—
That will be Nature too, something that rises
Out of the substance of my flesh as sure
As any vapor rising from the sheep,
But that will not be all, for we are here,
And what has happened on this road is ours.

So, of these walls that stood a hundred years
And now are going back to something we
Believe we have begun to understand,
And of the slow feet that made good this road,
And of the beaver hands that made these walls,
I speak new words, to last until they change,
And when my song is lost, if someone says:
It ought to be restored,
                         let someone lift
One handful of this earth and say:
                                It is!

Fort Laramie

Skylike grew delphiniums
Through the planking cracks in the two-inch floor;
This is Wyoming walking in,
I said, through an open door.

Wyoming is old as a rotting plank
That is not humus yet,
Blue flowers walk through an open door,
They grow through puncheons in the floor,
Petals blow on the trapper's hearth.
Under this floor and in the earth,
I said, is a taproot net,
And the roof is a thing the sun shines through
To make Wyoming flowers blue.

I touched the frame, there was no door,
It was a place where a door had been;
I said there was a time before
These bluest flowers came walking in
When such a quiet opening
In a strong wall in the afternoon,
With no one here and a strong door gone,
Would have been a fearful thing.

(I said Cheyennes and Sioux left more
Than silent flowers upon a floor.)

I watched the pigeons roar and pound
And drag their tails upon the ground,
And I said these walls are thicker than
The arm's length of a prairie man,
But I said a pigeon circles through
These four white walls of stony mud
As if no smoky pane had ever
Turned the sun to pigeon's blood,
I said does anyone recall
When birds did not fly through this wall?

My hand touched the bud of a blue flower's coming
And I heard a pigeon's mating drumming;
What is Fort Laramie? I said,
There flows the Platte, here are the dead:
They lie in a fold of the greasewood ground,
A few were killed and some were drowned,
And some had reasons for knowing why
Any place was a place to die,
And I looked to see if any stone
Said *Better die here than in Oregon,*
And I looked for letters that could be pieced
Into *We died here on our way back East.*

But I found no words from the honest dead
For the living had marked the stones instead.

Lone men grow honest when they die,
You can sometimes tell by the way they lie
Where they were going and why they stopped,
But these, I said, have all been propped
In cottonwood boxes of compromise
With coppered eyes on paradise
And backs set tight against the world,
With arms well crossed and fingers curled;
How many death-set arms were cracked
To build a sign the living lacked?
How many honest muscles sprung
To fit a hymn that must be sung?
What is a cross upon a breast
That does not face the East or West,
Here under me
At Laramie?

Fort Laramie is Nature now:
I said if there is any trace
Of how many millions passed this place
Under canvas tilts with faces drawn
On the bitter dream of Oregon,
Then any man is natural
As a prairie dog or a coral thing
Or a wind that blows a mountain down.

Bill Sublette was a coral thing,
This is your reef, too, Broken Hand;
Bob Campbell was a prairie dog,
This is your mound of earth, Bob Campbell;
Jim Bridger was a blowing wind,
This is a mountain's bone, Old Gabe;
Kit Carson, did you write a will?
This graveyard, Kit, is also Nature;
Dreamers, fighters, cowards, lovers,
Here is a plank a blossom covers,
Here is Wyoming walking in
With a blue flower and a pigeon's wing.

Two Rivers

Two rivers that were here before there was
A city here still come together: one
Is a mountain river flowing into the prairie;
One is a prairie river flowing toward
The mountains but feeling them and turning
  back
The way some of the people who came here
  did.

Most of the time these people hardly seemed
To realize they wanted to be remembered,
Because the mountains told them not to die.

I wasn't here, yet I remember them,
That first night long ago, those wagon people
Who pushed aside enough of the cottonwoods
To build our city where the blueness rested.

They were with me, they told me afterward,
When I stood on a splintered wooden viaduct
Before it changed to steel and I to man.
They told me while I stared down at the water:
If you will stay we will not go away.

Words for Leadville

By the brewery pond in California Gulch
A blind man taught me how to slit a trout
And gut it with my thumb.
                     A dead fish squeaks.
That I remember and the old man's thumb,
The thumbnail cracked with dynamite and granite;
A mountain had exploded in his eyes.

I smelled the spruces and the shadow of
Mount Massive on the brewery, and I saw
The lights of Leadville, and I passed my hand
Through drops of yellow water dripping from
A wooden flume into the yellow roses.

You can't get out, the mountains are so high,
You have to stay in Leadville till you die.

They called me in to supper: there were prayers,
And marmalade and venison and oysters—
  "We thank Thee, God, for these, Thy bounteous
    gifts"
And polished lamps and perfumed ladies rustling,
And gentle bearded men and bright nasturtiums,
And there was beer and trout and cheese and milk.

One day long afterward up here I asked
Four people where the brewery used to be.
They didn't know, but I found where it was:
Part of a fence was left and a briar rose.

It was a quiet Leadville Sunday morning:
The empty mountains, inside out, so still
You couldn't even hear the crackle of
The wooden props that tried to hold them up.
They looked like heaps of poked-up panther skins,
Stretching and sagging, yellow in the sun.

The city that had slid into the valley
Had settled in a pattern for an hour,
Most of the steeples pointing toward the sky.
The motorcars of tourists late to bed
Were white with frost wherever there was shadow,
But dripping where the sun struck the enamel.

The dusty tires were cool, you couldn't see
The stains of gentians nor the blood of chipmunks.
The whores were sleeping with their shades pulled down:
The tame coyote that one had in her window
Yawned when I tapped at him, as if a tap
From the outside of the window had no meaning.
A man who no one seemed to think was dead
Lay in the walk with flies about his lips;
I stepped across him as the others did,
All on their way uphill to the tolling churches.

It's uphill to the Wolftone mine,
It's uphill to the Matchless mine,
It's Sunday in the Terrible,
It's Sunday in the Chrysolite,
It's Sunday in the Waterloo.
The angels count the sparrow bones
In the Pittsburgh mine and the Printer Boy,
It's Sunday dripping in the Yak.
The angels count the sparrow bones
In the Mike and the Resurrection.

    "We thank Thee, God, for these, Thy bounteous gifts."

*   *   *

I walk alone up Harrison Avenue
Remembering . . . remembering myself . . .

But I remember more than I remember:
The blood of time, the wincing of the earth,
The spasms of the ranges wrinkling down
Into the silver crucibles of lead,
Gold in the burnt rock, gold in the water sands,
Gold in the tangled roots of purple currants.
Wasn't I there then?
    Something?
        A timber thing
When August dried the velvet in the antlers
Of a thousand centuries?
       When sloths were cool?
When lightning nicked the smell of ivory smoke
From April mastodons?
       How slow the beasts
To crumble golden pathways through this quartz!
How slow the generations of the fish
Rubbing their autumn bellies on this gold,
Fish in the slurry choking floods of spring
Clogging their crimson gills with tumbling gold!

The gold lay still so many afternoons
So blue, so cold, so cold in summertime
The nutcrackers could see their cawing frozen,
And many elephants had turned to stone
And many fish to shale before the day
When Abe Lee hollered seven hundred miles:
 "By God! I've got all California
 Right here in this here pan . . ."
A goose quill full of gold!
A coffin full!
Acres of slopping gold!
Oceans of gold!

 "By God! My wife can be a lady now . . ."

Opera houses slopping down the flumes!
Whisky slopping over the riffle blocks!
Railroads! Moonlight! Diamond-studded garters!
Necks for nooses! Smelters! Homes for orphans!
Gold for a snowshoe priest and a quart of milk!
For colleges! For jigsaw senators!
Surgeons! Orchids! Bells for monasteries!
Mirrors for the ceilings of the brothels!

 "Now by the golden mirrors in this room
 Your flesh can love me more than you can love me . . ."

Moonlight sliding over the riffle blocks!
Warm pneumonia over the riffle blocks!
Blood on the sawdust floor and a whisky cry:

"We'll all go back and join Abe Lincoln's army!"

And seven hundred miles away the brides
Are chanting on the banks of the Missouri:
"When shall we come?"
                              "Come when the grass begins!"

                    *   *   *

Deep in the rocky pages of the hills
Like bookmarks, lilies of the sea are printed.
A sleepy woodchuck winters in the earth,
Nosing his way through lilies petrified
And seams of country rock and porphyry . . .
He curls against a frozen tide of *silver!*
Bonanza silver!
          Silver!
                    Silver bullion!

The carbonates are clanging like a bell!
The mountains ring, the mountains swing!
The clappers of the mountains crack!
The silver cracks
And the single jacks
And the hammers bang,
And the hair grows long
And the ear is thatched
To hold a match as dry as bone
To light a fuse to crack the stone!

The whipsaw buckles in the pitch,
The bright axe chops and slits and chops,
The wood tick stops and runs and stops,
The log chain hooks a jangled hitch.
They tug at logs, the roaring men,
The frightened men, the coughing men;
The sweating salt is caking on
The tenderness behind their knees,
Sweating resin oozes noon
Out of the wounded trees.

With midnight whisky in their skulls
They drag the bloodshot forest down,
The mortise, chip and spike and lock
The forest underneath the town,
The giant powder nausea roars
Through rooms and tombs with silver floors.

Fifteen acres rib a mine,
Yellow gold to the Yellow pine,
Silver spruce to the silver ore,
The bristlecone shall drip no more
The long rain down its needles.

Logs to rib the Congo Mine,
Logs to rib the Yellowjacket,
Logs to rib the Dunderburg,
The Dome, the Law, the Iron, the Hope,
The sallow joinery of lungs . . .
     "Oh Christ! I want to get out of here!"
Smuggler, Oro, Little Eva,
Yankee Doodle . . .
                    Gone Abroad!

Logs for a stamp mill tom-tom all night long,
Tom-tom drums for a can-can dancer's grunt,
Can-can drums for a tin-horn gambler's clink:
     "I'll bet my moccasins!"
     "I'll bet my squaw!"
     "My pick, my candle butts, my fuse, my pork!"
     "I'll bet a dollar!"
     "Fifty thousand dollars!"
     "By God! I'll bet my banks!"
     "I'll bet my smelters!"
                    * * *
Horn silver?
               Blossom rock to flower again?
Their fingers tweak the last wick into smoke.
The dancers flicker down.
                         The cut-glass planets
Have tightened Tiger Alley into frost,
And Stillborn Alley squeaks like rats that squeak
Against the starry fetus on the dump . . .

No larkspur for you, child, no gates to open,
Never to live and love until it hurts,
Never returning, never being sleepy . . .

The miners go to sleep remembering
The hog kettles of home. They go to sleep
On beds of juniper remembering
The nests of wasps that hang from far-off ridgepoles,
A well sweep and a face and a mullein stalk,
The smell of hay-juice caking on a scythe,
Remembering preachers and the thighs of women.

The miners sleep so deep they do not wake;
The miners change to angels playing harps,
They sing along the golden streets of heaven.
The stakes they drove into the crusted snow
To claim the bitter nodules of the flint
Are washed away. The shining foil is gone.
The earth so sour behind the cabin door
Is sweet with raspberries and sweet with roses.
The old squaws chatter up the long blue trails,
They change to ghosts that rattle plum-stone dice.

*   *   *

The lobes of glaciers melt. The deep mines fill
With water inching upward black and still,
The cobwebs bind the windlass at the top,
The plumb-line spiders dangle till they drop.

I stroke my palm across the frozen slag.
What latch to lift?
                     What step to take uphill?
The ranges fold the hay into their blueness,
The blossoms drip with night, the planets rise
Into the ordered schedule of my hunger
For what has been, continues, and will be.

Yet this I tell you. This is practical
Against whatever custom in your heart
There is for shaping ruins into thresholds:

Here is a town with houses tenanted,
Here is a town with silent houses crumbling,
If you are overtaken, they are shelter,
If you are cold, their splinters will make fire,
If you are rich, there will be purple asters,
If you are poor, there will be purple asters,
And if you are resourceful you can file
A silver dollar to a cutting edge,
And cut, not one, but any hundred asters,
Saying:
    "I cut a hundred purple asters,
    Using a knife I made out of a dollar!"
And if you have a watch, your watch will tick,
And you can count the beatings of your heart,
While roots of ferns are splitting particles
Of time from granite and the corpuscles
Of blood within you alter their confusion
A tombward instant irrevocably.

Morning Star

It is tomorrow now
In this black incredible grass.

The mountains with luminous discipline
Are coming out of the blackness
To take their places one in front of the other.

I know where you are and where the river is.

You are near enough to be a far horizon.
Your body breathing is a silver edge
Of a long black mountain rising and falling slowly
Against the morning-and the morning star.

Before we cannot speak again
There will be time to use the morning star
For anything, like brushing it against
A pentstemon,
Or nearly closing the lashes of our lids
As children do to make the star come down.

Or I can say to myself as if I were
A wanderer being asked where he had been
Among the hills: "There was a range of mountains
Once I loved until I could not breathe."

Ghost Town

Here was the glint of the blossom rock,
Here Colorado dug the gold
For a sealskin vest and a rope of pearl
And a garter jewel from Amsterdam
And a house of stone with a jig-saw porch
Over the hogbacks under the moon
Out where the prairies are.

Here's where the conifers long ago
When there were conifers cried to the lovers:
    Dig in the earth for gold while you.are young!
Here's where they cut the conifers and ribbed
The mines with conifers that sang no more,
And here they dug the gold and went away,
Here are the empty houses, hollow mountains,
Even the rats, the beetles and the cattle
That used these houses after they were gone
Are gone; the gold is gone,
There's nothing here,
Only the deep mines crying to be filled.

You mines, you yellow throats,
You mountainsides of yellow throats
Where all the trees are gone,
You yellow throats crying a canyon chant:
  Fill what is hollow;
Crying like thunder going home in summer:
  Fill what is hollow in the earth;
Crying deep like old trees long ago:
  Fill what is hollow now the gold is gone;
Crying deep like voices of the timbers,
Conifers blowing, feathered conifers,
Blowing the smell of resin into the rain,
Over the afternoons of timber cutters,
Over the silver axes long ago,
Over the mountains shining wet like whipsaws,
Crying like all the wind that goes away:
  Fill what is hollow,
  Send something down to fill the pits
  Now that the gold is gone;
You mines, you yellow throats,
Cry to the hills, be patient with the hills,
The hills will come, the houses do not answer.

These houses do not answer any cry.
I go from door to door, I wait an hour
Upon a ledge too high to be a street,
Saying from here a man could throw a rock
On any roof in town, but I will wait:
It's time the people came out of their houses
To show each other where the moon is rising;
Moon, do you hear the crying of the mines:
Fill what is hollow,
Send down the moonlight?

It's time the people kindled evening fires,
I'll watch the chimneys, then I will go down;
Steeple, why don't you ring a bell?
Why don't you ring a mad high silver bell
Against the crying of the yellow throats?
Wait for me, steeple, I will ring the bell.

    Pull the rope,
    Drift, stope,
    Pull a fathom of rock
    And a cord of ore
    From the higher place to fill the lower,
    The Rocky Mountains are falling down,
    Go into any house in town,
    You can hear the dark in the kitchen sing,
    The kitchen floor is a bubbling spring,
    The mountains have sealed like the door of a tomb
    The sliding doors to the dining room;
    Then thump your hand on the parlor wall
    And hear the Rocky Mountains fall,
    Feel the plaster ribs and the paper skin
    Of the Rocky Mountains caving in;
    Pull the rope,
    Drift, stope,
    Pull down the birds out of the air,
    Pull down the dust that's floating where
    The conifers blew the resin rain,
    Pull all the mountains down again,
    Pull the steeple down
    And a cord of ore
    To fill the dark
    On the hollow floor.

I am an animal, I enter houses.
Some of the animals have liked this house:
The first to come and go were men,
Men animals who dreamed of yellow gold,
Then small things came and the cattle came.
The cattle used this room for many years,
The floor is level with the baseboard now,
But probably the ants came first
Before the people went away;
Before the children wore the sill
With stepping in and out to die;
It may have been an afternoon
Before the conifers were dead,
An afternoon when the rain had fallen
And the children were going back to play.
You children going back to play,
Did you ask the things the animals can't ask?
Did you ask what made the mountains glisten blue?
Did you say: "The great wet mountains shine like whip-
    saws"?
Did you say: "We're here and there's the sun"?
Did you say: "The golden mines are playing
Yellow leapfrog down the hills"?
Did you say: "Think what it would be like
To be way up on the mountain top
And see how beautiful it is
To be where we are now"?

The children made this doorstone look
Like a whetstone worked too hard in the center,
And the ants went out and the wall went out,
And the rats went out and the cattle came,
But they're gone now, all the animals;
If they were here, and all of us together,
What could we say about the gold we dug,
What could we say about this house we used,
What could we say that we could understand?

You men and women, builders of these houses,
You lovers hearing the conifers at night,
You lovers making children for the houses,
Did you say to yourselves when reckoning
The yield of gold per cord of ore,
Running drifts per cord of ore,
Stoping per fathom per cord of ore,
Filling buckets per cord of ore,
Dressing tailings per cord of ore—
You lovers making children in these mountains,
Did you say something animals can't say?
Did you say: "We know why we built these houses"?
Did you say: "We know what the gold is for"?

I cannot tell: you and the gold are gone,
And nearly all the animals are gone;
It seems that after animals are gone,
The green things come to houses and stay longer;
The things with blossoms take an old house down
More quietly than wind, more slow than mountains.
I say I cannot tell, I am alone,
It is too much to be the last one here,
For now I hear only the yellow throats
Of deep mines crying to be filled again
Even with little things like bones of birds,
But I can hear some of the houses crying:

"Which of the animals did use us better?"
And I can hear the mountains falling down
Like thunder going home.

Three-Cornered Fern

Once in the black gorge under Estabrook
I stopped to rest and wondered what was lost
In the terrible water tumbling, never ending
Its awful definition of my body.

A star came on the hour or so I waited
Until I saw my father climbing up
As if he were working out of a waterfall
With movement more discernible than form.

I called to him, he saw me and called back,
He stopped, I thought it might be too much for him,
He called again and pointed to a rock:
It was the clump of oak fern we remembered.

Nothing Is Long Ago

Here in America nothing is long ago:
George Washington was never in Oregon,
He never saw a Flathead woman flop
Her breast across her shoulder to a child,
He never saw the stranded cedar bark
Blow from her salmon thighs like a weaver's thrums.

But it wasn't long:

                  The corn came quick enough
For Buffalo Bill to eat it out of a can
In a barber shop in a circus tent in London.
You used to see the old man hanging around
The City Desk as if it were a bee tree.

We cut the trees so quick for planting corn,
Your grandfather on the wall had time to push
A lever on a morning-glory trumpet:

The-Ed-dis-son-ree-kaw-ding-awk-kes-straw
with-elephants-with-elephants-with-elephants
to-ride-upon-my-little-Irish-Rose . . .

Nothing is long ago when you hear a saw:
It cuts so quick the centuries of pitch
The seasons wrap in rings around a tree,
The trunk will scream in two before your eyes,
Before your lips can move enough to say:

Is it the whine of a soggy witch in Boston?
Is it a cut slave shrieking like a bob-cat?
Is it a woman splitting in Missouri
to give a man child to the Rocky Mountains?

Old Men on the Blue

I know a barn in Breckenridge on the Blue,
In Summit County, Colorado, where
A Ford transmission rots upon the wall
Beside an ox-yoke. You can stand inside
The barn and peer like a pack-rat through the logs
And see how summertime looks outdoors, and see
A sleigh with hare-bells ringing under it,
And snowy yarrow drifting over the runners.

How high the mountains are behind the barn
Along toward evening nobody seems to know,
And nobody seems to know how blue they are,
Not even the old men sitting all day long
On a ledge in the shade in front of the general store;
But they watch the gasoline go up and down
In the big glass pump where the white-faced people stop
Who are crossing the Rocky Mountains.

They watch the white-faced people crawl away
Into the hackled fractures of the peaks,
Up where the Mississippi River ends
And the bodies of the frozen dragonflies
Begin to float to the Gulf of California.

The mountain ranges in the evening fill
The sockets of the old men's eyes with blue,
And some of their cheeks are lavender and lilac.
One long day after sunset sunlight poured
Out of the east, from an amber thunderhead,
To make their cheek-bones shine like yellow gold.

The old men do not speak while the pump is running,
But when you drive away you can hear their voices,
Like sounds you hear alone at night in a canyon
When pieces of blackness clatter on pieces of water,
And you think if you didn't have the car in low,
You could overhear what the mountains have never told
    you.

At night the old men sleep in houses that
Will always have geraniums in the windows.

This Lake Is Mine

Spaniel and stick, I walk around a lake
In City Park in Denver, Colorado.
We walk an hour: an hour's an increment
Of history to any hickory stick,
Or town, or boy, or ghost, or lake of water.

This lake is mine: this popcorn gravel edge
Of water holding brass band overtures
And willow roots and carp and lilac roots,
And rumbling lightning thunderheads behind
The music-nudging rowboats and the swans;
And black behind the arc lights are the beasts,
The wolves, the stagnant bears, the city panthers,
But never a sound comes from the nodding bison
Dragging the gold-braid music through their beards.

There is a bell that calls the rowboats in
At evening's end and girls in organdy
And young men wearing flannel trousers come
To shore remembering the inland click
Of water in the willow-drooping places,
And lilac panther cries and far-off waltzes.

No other water ever smelled like this.
I was a little boy: I knew the feel
Of crisscross sleepy benches pinching green
And the blare of the beautiful beautiful big brass horns,
Then mother saying: "Come, we're going home . . ."
Home was a black direction toward the beasts,
Home was a sleepy flavor in your mouth
Through cottonwoods to a yellow trolley car
With window sills that tasted of varnished varnish.

No other water ever was so still,
So still for grappling hooks engaging death.
Remember how she looked?
                              The broken garter?
The angled wrist? The dripping willow plume?
The high-laced patent-leather boots with tassels?
The amber-shining thigh?
                              It was a woman.
Women have legs but they are not like ours.

No other water ever was so quick
For making willow bark for knives to cut.
"What promise shall we keep, we've made so many?"
The willows walk away. They change their places.
"Which was our tree? I thought the tree was here."
"Of course I love you. Why do you keep asking?"

No other water ever was so slow
For making pines grow taller than a boy.

II

Now while I stroke these rushes with my stick
And chew this bitter twig of almond willow,
I see the blue bow of the Rocky Mountains
Bending around my city to the west,

Bending from Yucatan to arctic roses,
And spanning in one single summer's day
All seasons: springtime, summer, autumn, winter.
It's quiet here, but if I hook my wrist
At arm's length I can cover with my hand
The rattling steeples of the jagged rock
Slitting the cotton paunches of the hail.

Here it is lilac time, one kite still flying.
I follow the kite-string up the sagging sky
To crystal ranges where the pines as tall
As masts of ships are deep in summer snow,
Their tips a finger's length above the crust,
Like cotyledons in a glacial garden.
Against the violet ice I can discern
The spruces bristling on the lower hogbacks,
Like hairs of iron a horseshoe magnet drags
From little sand-pile mountains in a schoolyard.

So I go dreaming up a bellied kite-string
Into the old economies of water . . .
The dripping of the summer-inching glaciers,
The water trickling down this continent,
The water bringing beaver hunters back,
The water sluicing gold out of the mountains,
The water bloating oxen into gas,
The water changing cottonwoods to cities,
The water climbing lattices of clay
Into the root hairs of the grama grass.

The air is clear for seeing snow too far,
And I could tell the boy who flies the kite:
We are the lizards panting in the saltweed,
We are the gasping fish, the wilted larks,
The wetted finger hissing to the plowshare,
We are the dust that turns the sun to blue
Over the blistercress, the soda places;
And I could tell the boy who flies the kite
About the yellow cactus blooming here
Before this lake was here or we were here.

I lie upon my belly on the grass,
I whisper names of motorcars that glide
Reflected upside down among the fish . . .
De Soto, Hudson, Cadillac, La Salle,
The river men, the frosty men uphill,
I whisper names that are the names of ghosts . . .
Fitzpatrick, Lisa, Jedediah Smith,
Mackenzie, Coronado, Ogden, Hearne,
Singing the long song to the nameless mountains.

Where is the yellow gold, the fur, the amber?
Which is the river to the Seven Cities?
How far beyond the sunset are the mountains?
What mountain river flows into Cathay?

The snows have melted questions into answers,
The river singers slowly change to water:

Bill Ashley is a waterfall in Utah,
And Father Escalante is a river,
John Hoback is a river in Wyoming,
John Day's a river out in Oregon,
Kit Carson is a river in Nevada,
Bill Williams flows into the Colorado,
Jim Bridger is a lake that turns no wheel.

Some of the dead are water . . .

And my stick,
From walking far and changing histories
Of little things like ants on rainy flagstones,
Is blunted at the end.

I whirl the stick.
I scar the lake, a sweeping shoulder stroke.
The drops of water splash into the gravel,
And there are lenses, if I needed them,
For altered history within one drop
Alive with lucid water animals
That perish on my shoe in sunlight warm
As sunlight sloping down the afternoon
The river namer, old Bill Williams, died,
Sunning himself, his back against a tree,
Somewhere in mountains no one knows about.
Maybe it helps, or ought to help, to think
Of microscopic water animals
And old Bill Williams drying in the sun,
As giving angel-like advice to us,
Telling us:

Hurry! There is time to throw
Your stick into a high box-elder tree
To bring a winged samara spinning down!

Yet if you do not need a spinning seed,
Or only seed and not the spinning down,
You may have other uses for the time
It takes for not yet being dead . . .

                                        Or loving.

                    III

The time it takes for not yet being dead
Is ticking in the watches in the pockets
Of people stopping cars beside this lake.
They come here to make love. They're not molested.
The motor runs a moment longer here
And stops as if it were not planned to stop.
It's not too dark to see a flying bird,
Yet dark enough for the wrist that turns the key
To turn the woods on on the other side.
They look like woods. Love tries to make them woods.

The lake is clouding as a mirror clouds.
There's naked silk against the gear-shift lever
And light comes from the wrong part of the sky
To make lips redder than the blood that burns
Into their upward-stroking syllables.

I snap my fingers and the lake is older,
The lids of eyes are older, and the lips;
The hairspring in a watch is measuring
The jerking in the muscles of a heart;
The grass is working and the trees are working,
The anther working and the needle pumping,
The heart is pumping and positions change:
A carp has crossed the shadow of a duck,
And deep within the dark mechanics of
A willow leaf tomorrow gropes for use.

Positions of the lovers change and change,
The knee, the wrist, the spine, the cheek, the thigh,
The eyes are open and the eyes are closed,
The muscles of the lips and tongues and throats
Make air make sounds: *I love you! I adore you!*

They hardly see the raindrops on the windshield,
They hardly see the evening on the fenders,
They hardly see a misty circling bird.

I know this bird that circles rainy water,
All silverness like dust of aspen bark:
Its name is Forster's tern, a random thing
Intent on fluttering in no direction;
But if I fix a sight-line from my stick
Across the water to some mountaintop,
The random bird will intersect the line,
Winging the very space he used before.
It may be fins that brings him back to fish,
I only know the circling bird returns.

The silver bird the lovers hardly see
And hardly need returns long afterward . . .
Over the helix hairspring of the years,
Over the lake unfinished, love unfinished,
And I can hear a lonely whisper saying:

It must have been . . . because I can remember
The way the water looked, and I remember
The mountains and the rain against the willow,
And I remember how a silver bird
Flew over us and over us and over us . . .

So is there need for hills behind a face,
And wings against the transitory hills,
So would I take one cooling summer locust
Into my heart to sing beyond erosion;
And if I say this night to you, my lover:
    "The locusts are asleep," my heart is saying:
    "God bless you, but if Time outlive our God,
Time bless you, dear . . ."
                                I whistle to my dog.

Some Grass

I will not name this grass,
I did not know its name when I was younger,
Then there was more than summer for a boy
Who walked in it with fingers and with hunger.

It is not meadow grass,
But prairie city where the flagstone courses
Along a place where no one built his house
And I remember seeing tethered horses.

It is not grass alone:
Between the flagstone and the curb there grows
Thistle and lambsquarter and some wild thing
That was and is like mint against my nose.

I will not pull this grass,
I have too many dollars in my pocket,
Or not enough, there is no way of telling;
I dare not pull a green beard from its socket.

It is not grass alone,
Or I would cross the street less often than
I do to see it, yet it may have been
Much more like grass before I was a man.

Streets Due West

The end of every street a hill,
The top of every hill a line
Too indistinct in blue and blue
For any to divine,
Were just as strange as any street
That ended in a gleaming sail,
Or any wall ten chariots wide,
Sung in a golden tale.

All streets end in morality
Of fables told in human span,
Where three score years and ten are roofs
And spires to measure man,
Save these that end in blue and blue,
In peak and peak and sky and sky,
At seven on an April night,
Immeasurably high.

House in Denver

I can remember looking cross-lots from
This house over the evening thistle and
The bee flowers, watching people coming home
From downtown. In the morning I could stand
A long time watching my father disappear
Beyond the sunflowers which you noticed farther
In the morning. Now tall buildings interfere
In piles of shining masonry, but are there
Walls yet to come no more secure than these?
My city has not worn its shadows long
Enough to quiet even prairie bees.
I often hear a droning sunflower song
Dissolving the steel, and mark a thistle turning
A curling wall back when I'm thistle burning.

This Foreman

"What did you see when girders rose?"
"A house of steel, a net."
"What else?"
    "Men in their working clothes,
Men with their foreheads wet;
I saw them sway on the high steel beams,
But I knew their heads were wet."

"Did you see a workman slip and fall dead?"
    "I saw one leave the steel;
I heard what some of the others said,
And I saw the swallows wheel
Round the foreman with the twisted head,
Whose foot was half a heel."

"When the man fell, what did this foreman do?"
    "He sang, he sang like a swan
Of how two naked lovers loved
In a cage of steel till dawn;
He sang—and his mouth was a slit of dark—
Of a sword that could be drawn."

"You say you heard this foreman *sing?*"
  "I heard him sing like a swan."
"You say this foreman stopped to *sing*
When a man had fallen down?
(*He says he heard this foreman sing*
Like a swan when a man fell down.)"

"You heard this foreman testify?"
  "I heard each word he said."
"Now briefly what did the witness say?"
  "He said when the man fell dead,
He slid like a flash to the dead man's side
And gave the dead first aid."

"All right, now what did this foreman do?"
  "I heard him sing like a swan
About two naked lovers trapped
  In a web of steel till dawn."
"You swear to God you heard him *sing?*"
  "By God, that man's the one."

"Court please, I'll ask the witness more,
Court please, I wish to show,
Court please, the witness on the stand,
Court please, is trying to
Make light of what he saw and mock
The State, Court please, and you."
"Do you affirm that this foreman *sang?*"
  "I affirm that he's the one."

[134]

Now the bailiff hammers a terrible din,
But nobody shouts: Tin, tin, come in!
Because they all stare at the foreman instead,
Who licks the slit in his crooked head.

"You stayed there after twilight came?"
    "The twilight did not come;
The steel net shone like a russet flame
At the touch of the watchman's thumb;
The men went home and the watchman walked
His rounds slowly and dumb."

"All right, the twilight did not come;
You stayed, what happened then?"
    "I saw the foreman stealing back,
He climbed to the top again,
He moved in the misty girder net
And he sang like many men."

"Court please, I'll ask the witness more:
What did this foreman sing?"
    "He sang the strength of steel and steel
In days past measuring;
He tapped the beams with a monkey wrench;
I could feel the high crane ring."

"You're sure it was a monkey wrench?"
    "He sang of a snare for love;
He called to the silver hounds of love
In the wooded moon above,
And I heard him cry 'The hounds are dead,
What am I dreaming of?'"

"Go on, you heard this foreman sing?"
    "I heard him sing like a ghost,
How a man gone down was a man to lead
The van of a falling host:
    'Let my green steel stiffen in the frost
To snare what men love most!' "

"What men love most? He sang of that?"
    "I did not understand,
For he sang of the living lives of men
As if the steel had spanned
Their lives with something true and cold
That nobody had planned."

"Did your family know that you were there?"
    "Your honor, I object!"
    "Sustained!"
    "That's all."
    "Go down the hall to the last door and collect
Your fee . . . the last door on the right."
    "Poor chap, his mind is wrecked."

Two figures loitered down the hall,
And each signed for its fee.
    "I could not understand your song,
Explain the hounds to me."
    "Not here, fool! Climb the steel tonight,
The moon goes down at three!"

Can I Bring Home?

Can I bring home the actual spider-spun
Geometry to prove what silk-to-spruce
And silk-to-alder over my brook have woven?
Or hearing the vesper sparrow, can I use
Again the very cry and the very hues
Of day dissolving in his dark wet throat?
How can I hold the antelope I lose
So instantly above the yucca butte?
What seizures drive so hard? What inventory
Of our acquisitive thrift or studied plunder?
Yet what deep love runs deeper in our story?
Do we not say forever: Share my wonder?
Do we not say: Behold what I have seen
That we may love for loving where we've been?

Inner Song While Watching a Square Dance

Calico, cantle, scythe and snath,
Meadow, mountain, river path,
Swing on your corner like swingin' on a gate,
Now to your own if you're not too late,
The blood of you,
The blood of you
In every state:
Blood of your temple, wrist and thigh
Coursing imperceptibly
Wherever they stop at a filling station,
Wherever they beg to renew a note,
Wherever the sundown makes you love
And the new moon grips your throat.

Docie-doe your lipstick,
Swing your corner la-dee,
Promenade your cigarette
And swing her twice around!

Your Uncle Bill, he drove a drill
In the Moon Anchor mine in Cripple Creek,
Grandpa Amos scraped the hull
Of a windjammer three barnacles thick . . .

Promenade, O promenade,
Oregon and Everglade . . .

Agatha's shoes had toes of brass
That scuffed the sage in a mountain pass,
Aunt Sophronia, Mohawk Valley,
Uncle Pedro, Sacramento,
Uncle Horace, Broad and Wall,
Where sound conservative sparrows fall
On poor Aunt Cecil who fell in love
With a man who sold her a citrus grove,
And Barbara Jean and Shirley Mae
Were Flo and Polly yesterday,
(In the gloaming, O my darling . . .)
Flo and Polly yesterday,
Yesterday and yesterday,
Flavia, Persephone,
Eve and Lilith yesterday . . .

Buffalo gals will you come out tonight,
In the ilex grove,
In the lotos light,

Buffalo gals will you come out tonight
And stain your breasts with grape!

And the dance goes on
And the dance goes on,
The centuries go bare,
Go bare
As the color of wood where the paint is off
In a mountain town all falling down,

And they don't remember who it was
Put bleeding heart on the hose-cart hubs
For the fire parade, and briar rose,
Nobody knows and nobody knows
The pinch of parfleche moccasins
The night the bison hunt begins,
Or how it smells to trim a wick
Or how it feels to dust a lick
Of salt with the wing of a dappled hawk,
But around the ring you walk, walk, walk,
And you skip, skip, skip,
And you run, run, run,
And your permanent wave is melting down
And your white gardenia's edging brown,
One little two little three little injuns . . .
White gardenia edging brown,
Pale Comanches in the moonlight,
Pinto ponies in the moonlight,
Four little five little six little injuns . . .
Hurry, take my hand!

One little two little three little injuns . . .
Hurry, take my hand!

The white gardenia will not stay,
Her feet are far-off clover hay,
The gear-shift knob that molds her palm
Is long away,
Is long away,
Her hair is wind, her hair is gay,
He swings her twice around:
The phosphor of the ranges feels
The juice of cornlands in her heels,
Her throat has sung the seas apart
And all the hills are in her heart,
All the cities, every state . . .
Now to your own if you're not too late . . .
And the dance goes on
And the blood goes on
Till the constellations burn you down,
And O it's dark from here to town.

Noted

I have finished winter nearly,
Secretary to the stalks,
Wild blue lettuce, kinghead, yucca,
Sagebrush where my red mare walks.
Noted: sundown hurts a man,
Noted: planets fixed and frozen,
Noted: meeting on the plain
A dead man's cousin.
Noted: magpies need a glade,
Noted: by the time you touch
Any twig or grama blade
You have changed that much.
Noted of a cottonwood:
Hate could crack you down,
War is ever twice as near
As the nearest town;
Noted of a cottonwood:
Love can hold you ever,
Noted: willows tillering
From the frozen river.

Harper's Ferry Floating Away

I was riding on the B & O,
Great Cacapon to Sir John's Run,
A hundred miles from Washington,
I dozed,
I dozed by Sleepy Creek
And Cherry Run and Blairton . . .

I dozed a rhyme:
                                        I'd like to know
If light from the great star Fomalhaut
Is shining on Joe Aleck's place
Way out in Frannie, Wyoming . . .
The goldenrod brings Fomalhaut
And old Joe Aleck used to cook
For Grover Cleveland long ago . . .

I said and stopped the rhyme,

And the lounge car ticked the rails so slow
I thought the car was sliding back,
And ingots of the moonlight slid
Along the other track.

A magazine lay open on my lap
And I said to an air-conditioned Congo porter:
"Please let me know when we come to Harper's Ferry."

[143]

A meadow stitched with stubble scudded past,
I dozed the starlight down Joe Aleck's place,
The swing-glint of it over the Big Horn Mountains,
The swing-glint of it over the Absarokas;
I thought of Grandpa telling how old John Brown
Would hook one leg across the hominy block
And preach the birds off every tree in Kansas.

Harper's Ferry,
Harper's Ferry,
Me here,
Me here,
Almost Harper's Ferry,
Old John Brown about to stop the train,
Old John Brown about to free the slaves . . .

I read a folder to pass the time,
The folder made me make a rhyme:

The midnight B & O came in,
It whistled from the west,
Conductor Phelps he stopped the train,
A rifle at his breast;
The porter was the first to die,
They didn't understand
The reason why he tried to cross
The bridge to Maryland . . .
Swing low, sweet chariot,
Takin' Mister Hayward home . . .

How do you set a porter free?
How do you set a porter free?
John Brown tried and so do we:
Work or War or Dole or School?
God or Grab or Golden Rule?
How do you set a porter free?
Or set you free?
Or set me free?

The train rolled on about the time it takes
To wonder if the trout in the Beartooth Mountains
Strike or reject the ancient grasshoppers
That thaw as good as new from Grasshopper Glacier.

I opened my eyes,
I looked at the magazine,
A girl in the magazine crossed her legs at me
To try to make me buy a cigarette;
I saw the porter coming down the aisle:
Harper's Ferry,
Almost Harper's Ferry . . .

"Sorry, we jus' gone by," the porter said.
"Ah thought you woke up when ah pulled yo' coat."
"Sorry," he said,
"Sorry," like an amendment,
Grasshoppers floating away,
Harper's Ferry
Floating
Floating
Away . . .

"*Sorry?* Why should he be?" said the magazine,
"No class of workers in America
Is worse exploited than the Pullman porters!"

"But he really was," I said. "It was my fault
For dozing off . . ."
                              And the magazine exclaimed;
"You'd have the porter hollering *hallelujah*
Each time the whistle toots for Harper's Ferry?"

"Only," I said, "when you're in the thick of it,
And I mean *you* and not the porter now,
History implies a recognition . . ."

"Recognition of *what?*" said the magazine.
"Whatever gives you access to yourself,
Whatever gives you yesterday tomorrow,
Whatever . . ."
                              "Nonsense!" said the magazine.

"There's love in it," I said . . . "the land, the living,
And sometimes what your senses try to tell you
To keep the dead you want to live from dying:
John Brown's gone unless I want to keep him."
"The dead are dead!" observed the magazine.

I said: 'It's only chance it's Harper's Ferry.
Another day . . .
                              Kaskaskia or Sundance,
It might be Sitting Bull or Coronado,
It might be climbing a maple to whittle a whistle."

[146]

I thought of the taste of maple bark at the top
Of the tree on the Fourth of July,
Dick hollering up:

"Johnson just licked Jeffries!"
                    Old Dick dead:
Killing himself on the Coast and nothing working
In his poor dead skull any more if you stood on his grave
And tried to ask him:
                    Who was Ethan Allen?
If you tried to ask him:
                    Who was Stephen Foster?
Can you play *Susanna* on your mouthharp, Dick?
Dick, did you ever hear of old John Brown?
What's it like, Dick, smelling the Gunnison meadows?

The smell of gas lights in the Baptist Church?
And *Nearer My God to Thee* and mother saying:
"They played that at McKinley's funeral"?

"You're very silly," said the magazine.
I looked far back as I could up the Shenandoah,
These deep subaltern shadows of my land,
My people suffering,
My people shining,
Angels whispering to old John Brown,
Angels fingering his eye sockets . . .

The magazine kept talking, talking, talking:

There's nothing to this recognition nonsense,
The world is real and we are up against it,
My difficulty here at Harper's Ferry
Was one of simple ideology:
The John Brown thing was purely economic,
My old friend Dick, that's why he killed himself,
The economic cards were stacked against him.

I pressed my face on the windowpane of the valley,
The trees, the hills, the railroad tracks, the river,
The outer night so certain and unmoved
By wistful therapies men dream for men . . .

Answer me! Answer me! O strange Potomac!
I could imagine forbears back to Adam,
Archers, sailors, wanderers, herdsmen people,
And all their various troubled circumstance,
Not willfully to put me in this lounge car,
Not asking me to pay them any debt,
But putting me here . . .
The plasm of their passion,
Their very valent continuity.
The lover gasping *now* to the other lover,
The sexton saying *now* to the boy with a spade:

All nature saying nothing till we ask it,
Like me here now to ask a shagbark tree
Some invoicing of John Brown's clotted hair,
The scything of the heart,
The tedded blood,
The long long voice a prisoner about to be
The earth of earth again
Gives any wood lot.

The Gavel Falls

We had to leave the warm tidewater mud,
The warm-flanked wives, the estuary fish,
For an uphill dream and a trap in the beaver mist:

"Father said Cornwallis was very pale . . ."

We braided manes and tails of fallen horses
Into a harness tug a man could wear,
Monongahela, Niobrara, Paint Rock:

"You'll write me when you get to Sutter's River?"

We had to shout last wills and testaments
Over the wing-bone whistles of the Sioux,
We had to chant a cholera hymn to the willows,
We had to learn that beetles taste like acid
When no direction takes you anywhere:

"Cat's cradle, cat's cradle,
Skin of a broken boat . . ."
"All night we heard him singing rock-a-by tunes . . ."

And a love song in Virginia was a tomb
That sank into the grasses of Missouri:

"Four score and seven years ago our fathers . . ."

[150]

And a love song in Missouri was a tomb
That sank behind the mountains of the West:

  There was an American flag in the cedar tree,
  You could see it from the Osage orange hedge
  Where Grandmother shot the herons to feed the hogs,
  And after the war Grandfather paced all night
  Between the seven coffins in the orchard.

They brought Minerva's body home from Kansas,
Hiram came home from Missionary Ridge . . .
"Begone!" the old man shudders to the hound;
The slow hound turns away from Enoch's coffin.
Abraham sleeps. Lucinda coughs no more.

And the gavel falls!

The gavel falls on the sego lilies of Utah,
The gavel falls on Union Street in New Bedford
And the whaler's wharves at the end of Union Street
Can hear the gavel tapping gourds in Taos,
Tapping a taxicab fender in Atlanta,
Tapping the fossil pollens of Dakota,
Tapping the yellow smelter stack in Butte,
Sequoias, tugboats . . .
                    "Look! This came in the mail!"

The gavel is a change and a discipline:
    "They're going to hold the hearings at the school-
        house,
    The County Agent says we've got to be there!"
The gavel ends a dream and begins a dream:
    "The hearings, sir, are in the Venetian Room
    On the fortieth floor,"
                            and the schoolboy is a boaster:
    "Dad had to go to Washington! He flew!"

The gavel is a hunger for long peace,
The gavel is the faith and the prophecy
And a guttling drum and a bugler's booted cadence
And a mob all sweating salt to a fair messiah . . .
And the fruit flies roar with laughter at the gavel,
And the fruit flies sing absurd genetic songs
About the slow, slow human generations,
And the fruit flies scatter dice among the captains:
    "Caligula was a gentle child," they sing,
And they chatter incommunicable nonsense:
    "A bull snake may be thicker than the wrist
    Of an economist, but writes no poems."

So falls the oak leaf on the buffalo robe,
The far pung jingles into the maple bush,
The Pole Star slowly gives its place to Vega
And there's a farmer up at Custer, Montana:
The ants keep bringing beads to the top of the anthill,
They always have, and he doesn't know who it was.

Let Your Mind Wander Over America

Let your mind wander over America:
Be designated by a tumbleweed for tears
As if it were a flag.

Anything it can be, anywhere;
   Remember that marker down in Austin, Texas,
   When you were marching right front into line:
Thermopylae . . .
   (Influenza stacking coffins up
   Like cordwood on the railway station platform)
Thermopylae had her messenger of defeat,
The Alamo had none!

Let your mind wander, fluidly, freely,
Marker or meadow, something your mother told you
Not to be told of any other land,
Birds, bison, cornfields, Model-T's,
Brave men, cowards, songs you change for yourself
  Like the *Schwanda Polka and Fugue*, remember that
    one,
  Walking out of Carnegie Hall to find
  Where Aaron Burr and Theodosia lived,
  Whistling *Schwanda* twice around their square,
  Charlton Street, McDougal, Varick, King—
  How did I change a measure of the *Fugue*
  Into that crazy *Bird on Nellie's Hat?*
  Laugh with me, Aaron, we have something common,
  Pacing our sad steps to the river bank,
  Pistols waiting for us in Weehawken.

Let your mind wander, carelessly, I tell you,
Like the drone of a sycamore church through the
    hollyhocks:

  Count your blessings, name them one by one . . .

It's easier, I tell you, wandering that way
Than being told too hard, too tight, too quickly.
It will be gone if ever comes the time
For being told to love America.

Wander with herders, drovers, trail men, sailors,
For memory, desire, for wanting back,
Wanting back is how you name the future;
Wander into special sorrowings,
Wander into special differences
Of neighbor men, of heroes,
Legends known or half:

Once I was puzzling in the woods why no one
Seemed to remember hearing Lincoln sing
Or Washington laugh;
A bittern rose and flew above the trees
(Father called the bitterns thunder-pumpers)
And if I asked myself again somewhere
About that lack of song or lack of laughter,
My thunder-pumper could come in and after;
So do the strands, the fragments integrate
Till what you live for, die for, state by state,
Is willow-woven, winged, flavored, framed
By faces or by gallows trees you've named.

II

Oh not too large,
Be subtler if you like than cannon-fire
To know its meaning.

[155]

I'd tell you how even a summer dragonfly
Could hurt an old dead warrior's cheek three times
And mine a fourth
To make me feel the strong South bleeding hard
Against the North
And ice against the breast, Oh many a breast
Moving wintry West:

Maybe you never heard of General Dodge,
General Dodge was the man with the festered cheek,
He came out West to build the Union Pacific,
A bullet tore his cheek before Atlanta,
A rose thorn opened the same wound up in Boston
When Faneuil Hall was rocking to his glory
And a pale wild girl threw roses in his face,
And the cold sleet opened the same wound in Wyoming,
And at seventy at sundown in Wyoming
A dragonfly crashed through my open windshield,
It hurt my cheek so hard it wasn't mine,
For nine miles I was General Grenville Dodge
Moving against the vapors of the tempest,
Too cold to smell the stench of bison bodies,
Too far from camp to hear the Chinamen coughing,
The dragonfly against my cheek,
The sleet against the wound,
The rose, the bullet. . . .

What were you loving so to fire that bullet,
You Georgia bullet boy?
What were you loving so to throw that rose,
You pale wild Boston girl?
Why do I love you both long afterward
A russet autumn evening in Wyoming?

Out with you, broken dragonfly!
Your body incidental to the resin weed
Along the Lincoln Highway in Wyoming,
Along the Union Pacific in Wyoming,
Where Chinamen died and bison and Cheyennes,
Where palm trees died and elephants and fish,
Where oceans died and slowly changed to stone,
Your body incidental to the jessamine
Yellow for Georgia as this resin weed
Is yellow for Wyoming
Or as buttercups
Are yellow when the springtime's over Boston.

Concatenation or coincidence,
Foolish, personal, wise, yours, mine,
Let your mind wander over America,
Let your mind wander using more deeply than in **war**
Whatever blessed, blessed interval
Between the wars there is:

For if you go to war and come back whole,
There must be meaning in some gate you open,
And if you go to war and come not home,
There must be meaning in some gate you open.

To a Young Man Flying the Pacific

Reindeer herders watch you go,
Roaring shadow on the snow;
Jungle bird and coral flower
Hear you droning hour by hour.

There were reindeer in your book,
Borneo was in your book,
Burma was a name that meant
A golden cage in the animal tent.

Singapore was hard to spell,
China had a temple bell,
Oceans that you crayoned blue
Have come desperately true.

What meridians today
Are you crossing far away?
Arctic vapor, tropic mist
Ticking, ticking, on your wrist?

Here at home the suns go down
West of every eastern town,
West of every western place,
Sinking into ocean space . . .

Sinking to rise up behind you,
Suns we've blessed and told to find you;
Fused with dawn, you blaze a path
Of thunder-doom and blinding wrath

For huddled shores where squinting eyes
Of folly must behold the rise .
Of sun and sun and sun and sun
With agony for what was done.

No Mark

Corn grew where the corn was spilled
In the wreck where Casey Jones was killed,
Scrub-oak grows and sassafras
Around the shady stone you pass
To show where Stonewall Jackson fell
That Saturday at Chancellorsville,
And soapweed bayonets are steeled
Across the Custer battlefield;
But where you die the sky is black
A little while with cracking flak,
Then ocean closes very still
Above your skull that held our will.

O swing away, white gull, white gull,
Evening star, be beautiful.

Something Starting Over

You don't see buffalo skulls very much any more
On the Chugwater buttes or down the Cheyenne plains,
And when you roll at twilight over a draw,
With ages in your heart and hills in your eyes,
You can get about as much from a Model-T,
Stripped and forgotten in a sage arroyo,
As you can from asking the blue peaks over and over:
   "Will something old come back again tonight?
   Send something back to tell me what I want."

I do not know how long forever is,
But today is going to be long long ago,
There will be flint to find, and chariot wheels,
And silver saxophones the angels played,
So I ask myself if I can still remember
How a myth began this morning and how the people
Seemed hardly to know that something was starting over.

Oh, I get along all right with the old old times,
I've seen them sifting the ages in Nebraska
On Signal Butte at the head of Kiowa creek.
  (You can drink from the spring where old man
    Roubadeau
  Had his forge and anvil up in Cedar Valley,
  You can look back down the valley toward Scotts-
    bluff
  And still see dust clouds on the Oregon trail.)
I entered the trench they cut through Signal Butte,
And I pulled a buffalo bone from the eight-foot layer,
And I watched the jasper shards and arrowheads
Bounce in the jigging screen through which fell dust
Of antelope and pieces of the world
Too small to have a meaning to the sifters.

One of them said, when I held the bone in my hand:
  "This may turn out to be the oldest bison
In North America," and I could have added:
  "How strange, for this is one of the youngest hands
That ever squeezed a rubber bulb to show
How helium particles shoot through water vapor."
And the dry wind out of Wyoming might have
    whispered:
  "Today is going to be long long ago."

I know how it smells and feels to sift the ages,
But something is starting over and I say
It's just as beautiful to see the yucca
And cactus blossoms rising out of a Ford
In a sage arroyo on the Chugwater flats,
And pretend you see the carbon dioxide slipping
Into the poverty weed, and pretend you see
The root hairs of the buffalo grass beginning
To suck the vanadium steel of an axle to pieces,
An axle that took somebody somewhere,
To moving picture theaters and banks,
Over the ranges, over the cattle-guards,
Took people to dance-halls and cemeteries—
I like to think of them that way together:
Dance-halls and cemeteries, bodies beginning
To come together in dance-halls where the people
Seem hardly to know that hymns are beginning too;
Then bodies separating and going alone
Into the tilting uphill cemeteries,
Under the mesas, under the rimrock shadows.

I can look at an axle in a sage arroyo,
And hear them whispering, the back-seat lovers,
The old myth-makers, starting something over.

Index of First Lines

[168]